# THE
# CHRISTIAN'S
# HANDBOOK
# OF
# PSYCHIATRY

# THE CHRISTIAN'S HANDBOOK OF PSYCHIATRY

**O. QUENTIN HYDER, M.D.**

FLEMING H. REVELL COMPANY
OLD TAPPAN, NEW JERSEY

All Scripture quotations not otherwise identified are from the *King James Version of the Bible*.

Scripture quotation identified as PHILLIPS is from the *New Testament in Modern English* translated by J.B. Phillips, copyright J.B. Phillips, 1958.

Scripture quotation identified as WEYMOUTH is from the *New Testament in Modern Speech* by Richard Francis Weymouth.

Scripture quotation identified as WILLIAMS is from *The New Testament, A Translation for the People* by Charles B. Williams.

*SBN 8007–0472–X*

# CONTENTS

# FOREWORD

IT IS UNDERSTANDABLE why many Christians have shied away from psychiatry. The basic theories of the predominant Freudian therapy are hostile to the tried and proved concepts of the Bible. Fortunately, in recent years, a number of authorities have parted company with conventional psychiatry to present approaches more in harmony with sound Christian principles. An example is *Reality Therapy* by Dr. William Glasser.

Dr. O. Quentin Hyder has even more openly espoused and incorporated invaluable principles from the Bible to give psychiatry a new dimension. Worthwhile tenets of psychiatry have been selected and integrated with long proved directives of the Scriptures.

Therapists of all schools recognize that feelings of guilt can lead to serious types of neuroses and psychoses. Instead of seeking to neutralize these feelings with many expensive sessions of psychoanalysis, Dr. Hyder advocates the Scriptural method of freeing the mind from guilt. Instead of trying to treat the multifold symptoms induced by the *feelings*, he goes after the cause —guilt.

He cites his own experience when the Lord forgave and removed his burden of guilt. It was somewhat like the effect of tranquilizers and antidepressant medications. But there was a big difference—the relief was immediate, more dramatic, permanent, and devoid of hangovers.

9

He recognizes that a truly curative confession must be accompanied by "genuine inner repentance and change of heart." As a psychiatrist he sees more clearly than even some ministers do the importance of fortifying the cleansed mind with discipline. Because some Christians only nominally accept Christ, they never enjoy the abiding peace of mind that the entrance of His Spirit provides. As a result they suffer from frustration with ensuing disillusionment.

Dr. Hyder is too knowledgeable to perpetuate such superficiality. He shows that God is only obligated to give love, joy, and peace to those who yield themselves "in total surrender to His will." Only then can the common mind-disturbing *dis*appointments become *His*appointments.

Marital bickerings is another common symptom of mental disease too often affecting the entire family! Dr. Hyder not only focuses on the psychological factors involved but also shows the need for dealing with the spiritual problems of the husband and wife. Failure to include this needed catalytic agent accounts for the failures of counseling programs that are purely humanistic.

The average reader will appreciate the way the author clearly explains the psychiatric terms used. Also pastors, counselors, and parents will discover in this book many of the answers and methods of treatment that they always yearned for but never found. He also labels the mental disturbances that even people with limited knowledge can treat and also the more serious ones that should be referred to a psychiatrist without *any* delay.

He believes that many mental disturbances can be properly treated by psychiatrists who make no profession of religion. However, in certain situations a Christian psychiatrist is better qualified to treat the total man: body, mind, and soul. One chapter also gives helpful information showing where Christian psychiatrists can be located.

Readers of this helpful book should not be surprised if they differ with the author in a few of the many theological and psychiatric viewpoints expressed, but all must recognize the value and need of a book of this type. All should appreciate Dr. Hyder's training, experience, and genuine dedication to the Lord.

Here is not only a book but in it is also a gracious personality. The book is more like a helpful friend always available in time of need.

S.I.MCMILLEN, M.D.

# PREFACE

THE WORD *Christian* throughout this book is used in a very restricted sense. It does not mean anyone who is not Jewish, Moslem, Buddhist, or Hindu simply because he was born and raised in a nominally Christian family. It does not even mean someone who might call himself a Christian because he is a baptized and confirmed member of a church. It certainly does not include all those who have the attitude, "Even though I don't go to church I'm as good a Christian as he is"! The term *Christian* is used here solely to describe a man or woman who has made an individual commitment to Jesus Christ as his own personal Saviour and Lord. He believes that Christ sacrificed Himself for his sins, and that as a result of his accepting this after repentance as a full and sufficient atonement for sin, he has entered into an eternal relationship with Him. Generally such Christians believe in such essential doctrines as the divine inspiration of the Old and New Testament Scriptures, the virgin birth of Christ, His incarnation as God in human form, His factual historically authenticated resurrection from the dead, His ascension into the presence of God and His expected and hoped for coming again in glory. He believes that he will be empowered to live the Christian life and will be given love from God to enable him to love and serve his fellowmen.

For God hath not given us the spirit of fear; but of
power, and of love, and of a sound mind. (2 Timothy
1:7)

This book is written for committed Christians. It is intended to
help those people who would call themselves "born-again"
Christian believers and who, partly because of their personal
spiritual experiences, have difficulty understanding or accepting
the facts of mental illness or emotional disorders. Many have
believed that somehow their newfound relationship with God
should necessarily protect them from emotional illness, which is
regarded as sin or a punishment for sin. Many have also believed
that prayer, repentance, and Bible study, without human help,
can cure all such problems. Very often they can, but not always.
Sometimes God uses human means to aid His healing process.

Selfishness is the root cause of all sin, and the results of sin may
sometimes lead to personality or adjustment problems and some
neurotic, psychosomatic, or even psychotic conditions. This does
not mean that sin is the cause of all mental breakdowns or emotional disturbance. There are other causes which may be outside
the control of the sufferer.

It is not God's executive will that we become sick; but sometimes it is His permissive will. An unsound mind is just as much
a sickness as a broken leg or an acute appendicitis. Whereas many
Christians can accept a physical illness as being God's permissive
will and will seek help from a doctor, they cannot do so with
psychological or emotional problems. For these problems they
often believe man cannot help. Only the Holy Spirit can cure
them. "Why should this happen to me or to my loved one?"
"Why doesn't God answer my prayer and heal?" When emotional pain persists, as it can without treatment, this attitude leads
to a hopeless fatalism which can end in bitterness and loss of
faith.

No, Christians are not exempt, ". . . for He maketh His sun to rise on the evil and on the good, and sendeth rain on the just and on the unjust" (Matthew 5:45). We are just as vulnerable to emotional problems as non-Christians. The difference is that Christians have additional spiritual resources to rely on (see chapter 2) which can help to lead them out of fear and into power, love, and a sound mind. However, in addition to these spiritual resources there are the human resources of professional help and ordinary contact with Christian friends, both of which can help immeasurably. Perhaps God sometimes permits mental sickness to come into our lives, but He also provides some relief through human understanding, sympathy, encouragement, guidance, advice, and even medical treatment. The Christian has faith that there is a divine purpose in his suffering for an ultimate good which he might not understand this side of eternity, but this does not mean that he cannot use all means available to alleviate that suffering.

Not everyone who develops personal problems needs to go to a psychiatrist. Many can be helped adequately through pastoral counseling or through discussions with mature, concerned Christian friends. One of the main purposes of this book is to help Christians to understand the basic principles of mental and emotional illness so that they can know the extent to which they can help others in need and how they should do it. They can also learn when the troubles have come to the point where trained professional treatment is needed. These pages, then, provide helps for Christians to understand what they should do when confronted with suffering in their friends and loved ones.

"For God hath not given us the spirit of fear . . ." (2 Timothy 1:7). Some fear is necessary. Primitive man needed it for self-preservation. This is good, but then self-preservation led to selfishness, the root of all sin. Cain slew Abel, the supreme act of selfishness, the end result of mental illness. Jesus Christ died on the cross for you and me, the supreme act of unselfishness and the ultimate example of mental health. Fear is the opposite of love. Cain's fear of Abel led to murder. Christ's love for us led to eternal life.

". . . but of power, . . ." The power of the Holy Spirit is available to all believers. It is the greatest power in all of God's creation. It creates and sustains the entire universe and it is directly accessible through believing prayer. It can influence the mind and change the will and emotions of any who desire it. It can sustain and strengthen those who are afraid. "Fear thou not; for I am with thee: be not dismayed; for I am thy God: I will strengthen thee; yea, I will help thee; yea, I will uphold thee with the right hand of my righteousness" (Isaiah 41:10).

". . . and of love . . ." Love is giving—giving myself for the benefit of others. Love is unselfish—putting my needs below that of others. The ability to give unselfishly is one of the cardinal qualities of the person who is mentally healthy and emotionally mature. God gives us the ability to love. We must exercise it. "A new commandment I give unto you, That ye love one another; as I have loved you . . ." (John 13:34).

". . . and of a sound mind." The Greek word *sofronismos* literally means a straight, sober, or sane mind. Other modern translations have used such expressions as a well-balanced mind, sound judgment, self-control, self-discipline, or self-restraint. I like this emphasis on the responsibility of the self. A sound mind is a gift from God, but the self has to respond to it. As with all of God's gifts it has to be received and incorporated into one's self. If we do we will be able to go through this life at peace with man and God. It is a matter of faith. "Thou wilt keep him in perfect peace, whose mind is stayed on thee: because he trusteth in thee" (Isaiah 26:3).

O. QUENTIN HYDER

# ACKNOWLEDGMENTS

THIS BOOK is a product of twenty years of struggling to live the Christian life, fifteen of them as a physician. Many men and women have profoundly influenced me both spiritually and professionally. I owe them all a deep debt of gratitude though I can only mention a few here by name. I acknowledge first the influence of my parents, Dr. Roland I. Hyder and Dr. Louise S. Hobbs of Ipswich, England, who gave me the happy stable home in which I grew up and the inspiration to become a physician as they are.

Arthur H. Lewis, my tutor at Wellington College, England, more than anyone else inspired me to develop a desire to study, determination, and self-discipline. The Rev. E.J.H. Nash of Cambridge first spoke to me of a personal relationship with Christ, and the preaching, in Cambridge, of Dr. Donald Grey Barnhouse of Philadelphia persuaded me finally to enter into that relationship. Dr. D. Martin Lloyd-Jones, physician and preacher in London, greatly contributed to my spiritual growth, as did many friends who worshiped in assemblies of "Plymouth Brethren" both in England and the U.S.A.

Dr. Richard T. Shackelford of the Johns Hopkins Hospital in Baltimore helped me to establish myself in America and encouraged me to stay here. Dr. Donald Cole of Fuller Theological Seminary in Pasadena first interested me in Christian counseling, and Dr. Joseph Winston of Newport Beach, California, persuaded me to study psychiatry.

17

18                                                    *Acknowledgments*

I especially acknowledge my professors at the College of Physicians and Surgeons at Columbia University, New York State Psychiatric Institute, for all I learned from them through their lectures, books, clinical teaching, and personal communications: Dr. Lawrence C. Kolb, Chairman of the Department of Psychiatry, and Drs. Arthur Carr, Ronald Fieve, Shervert Frazier, Lothar Gidro-Frank, Lee Hall, Stanley Platman, and Philip Polatin.

Finally, I wish to express my sincere thanks to my pastor, the Reverend Roger Hull, Jr., for persuading me to give the lectures upon which this book is based; to my friend of many years Mrs. Daphne Baker for patiently transcribing the substance of them for my use as resource material; to my close friend and colleague Dr. Ira Silverstein for reviewing parts of the manuscript; and to my wife, Lou Ann, who suffered the inconvenience at home while I was writing it and who typed almost the whole manuscript for me.

O. QUENTIN HYDER

# THE
# CHRISTIAN'S
# HANDBOOK
# OF
# PSYCHIATRY

# 1
# INTRODUCTION: HISTORICAL SUMMARY

**Psychiatry and psychotherapy.**     Psychiatry is a medical specialty devoted to treating diseases of the mind and disorders of the emotions and behavior. As such there is no field of human endeavor by which psychiatry is not to some extent influenced. The whole subject overlaps considerably with psychology, or the study of the normal mind and personality, and with philosophy, sociology, anthropology, all natural and biological sciences, and with religion. The medical doctor who treats mental and emotional conditions is a psychiatrist and his technique is called psychotherapy. This is different from counseling in that a much more thorough attempt is made to understand the patient's psychopathology, or manifested symptoms, and his psychodynamics, which are descriptions of the connections between the causes of his illness and the effects they produce. Psychotherapy is similar to psychological or pastoral counseling in that they all are directed toward the goal of helping the patient to function more efficiently and to feel less emotional pain.

**Christian attitudes and mental illness.**     *Emotionality and mental effort in the normal Christian experience.*  The problem of the existence of mental illness has troubled Christian theologians and philosophers since the first century. There has always been difficulty in separating the psychological from the spiritual. This

21

is understandable since there is so much overlap. The Christian experience, especially that which involves a deep personal relationship with God in Christ, is a very emotional affair. Just as emotion is involved in a boy-girl or marriage relationship so it is involved in the intimate spiritual relationship between the believer and Christ. Sometimes in the intimate personal experiences of the devout Christian he becomes deeply involved emotionally, even to the point of tears, as his separation from his Lord by sin is followed by repentance leading to reconciliation. Intense emotion and intense psychological effort also are involved in the striving for expression of supplication and intercessory prayer which can lead to physical and mental exhaustion. Also, in moments of adoration, worship, and thanksgiving the Christian often experiences profound emotional involvement as his prayers carry him up into the spiritual realm. These are experiences he never had before he became a Christian. He is now an emotional and spiritual being whose every experience is potentially richer and more intense than before. Small wonder then, when the Christian becomes emotionally ill, that his illness is frequently complicated by his personal faith or his religious beliefs. A very common example of this is in the experience of depression.

*Harmful effects of depression on faith.* I frequently find when depressed Christians come to my office that their low mood, slowed-down thought processes and activity level, and general pessimism has led also to a loss of assurance of their salvation. Christians who have been saved many years and lived devoted lives of positive witness and strong personal testimony can lose their sense of closeness to Christ and their hope of eternal security. They believe they have sinned to the point where God can no longer forgive them, and they readily verbalize the fear that they were perhaps never really born-again in the first place.

They say they have lost their faith and feel separated from God. This erroneous belief compounds their pain and suffering. What is happening, however, is that their psychological depression is affecting their thoughts. The facts of history have not changed. Christ was crucified, is risen and coming again. The born-again believer is eternally numbered among the redeemed, but the depression he suffers causes him to lose faith in these facts. He relies on his feelings alone and these lead him astray. Let me illustrate how feelings, in denial of facts, can cause dangerous confusion.

*Necessity of adhering to the facts.* Some years ago I was piloting a small single-engined plane over London, and being somewhat braver than cautious I allowed myself to become trapped in some low rain clouds. My eyes lost sight of the horizon and my feet of course were not in contact with the ground. The only balance guides I had left were the semicircular canals in my inner ears, but these are not equipped to deal with the problems of spacial attitude without the assistance of either vision or touch. However, in front of me were the airplane's essential instruments, the turn and bank indicator, the artificial horizon, the climb and descent indicator, and others which gave me my air speed, altitude, and direction. By carefully watching these instruments I was able for a while to keep the plane flying straight and level. It required uninterrupted intense concentration, but eventually my attention wandered from them and I started relying only on my inner ear mechanism. I quickly wandered off course. I was lucky I didn't either stall and go into a spin or dive into the ground. It is literally possible, for example, if the instruments are not functioning properly and the pilot is tightly strapped in, for him to find himself flying completely upside down, in the wrong direction, or going down in a dive or spin. I was lucky that the cloud base was high enough off the ground for me not to fly into a building or a hill. As soon as I came down below it and saw the ground again, I knew I was safe.

We Christians are often like that in our daily lives, whether we are mentally ill or not. If we rely on our feelings, like the pilot relying on his own erroneous subjective information, we can pass through the dark clouds of life's disappointments and become completely disoriented and lose our faith. But if we keep our eyes on the instruments on the dashboard, the irrevocable facts of history and the person of Christ who is our guide and Master, we will progress straight and level through this life. "Let us run with patience the race that is set before us, Looking unto Jesus the author and finisher of our faith" (Hebrews 12:1,2).

*Both spiritual and human help are God's provision for suffering.* We must remember, however, that although it is indeed God's will for His children to be healthy, He sometimes temporarily permits suffering in various forms, either physical or emotional. There is a purpose for this which He will one day reveal to us, but during the period of pain and suffering He has provided two major sources of succor. Preeminently there is the power of the Holy Spirit mediated to us through prayer and searching of the Scriptures, and the deep intimate spiritual relationship between Christ and the suffering believer. Also, human help in the form of a counselor or psychotherapist is often part of God's provision for our need. My hope is that the remaining chapters of this book will give to the caring Christian, who desires to be used by God to help relieve emotional pain in those whom he loves, enough information to do all he can himself, and then refer the sufferer to those with special qualifications to do what is best possible within the scope of present human knowledge and understanding.

**Earliest concept of disease.**     Studies of primitive tribes today help to indicate that prehistoric man probably had the concept that all illnesses were caused by forces outside the body. These forces were usually regarded as supernatural, in the form of gods, demons, evil spirits, witches, or magicians. There were also healing gods to whom one could pray for protection and help.

**Egyptians.** Five thousand years ago the ancient Egyptians had healing gods such as Ra, the sun-god; Isis, the earth-goddess; and her hawk-headed son, Horus. His eye, worn as an amulet, evolved into today's "Rx" used on prescriptions, meaning recipe —imperative to receive. There was also Imhotep, probably the world's first physician, who centuries after his death was deified and worshiped by priest-physicians who studied medicine at temple schools in Memphis and Thebes.

The Smith papyrus, written during the seventeenth century B.C., referred to even more ancient documents and is considered the oldest surgical treatise in existence. In it we find the earliest mention of the brain; its anatomy is described and the correct observation is made that the functional results of a brain injury depended on which side had been damaged. The Ebers papyrus, only slightly later than the Smith, described eight hundred different diseases including the "wandering uterus" from which we get, via the Greek *hysteros,* our word *hysterical.* The Egyptians were aware of the power of suggestion, and religious incantations were used by magician-priests to give patients peace and confidence and thereby enhance recovery from physical and mental illnesses.

**Assyria and Babylonia.** The Assyrians taught medicine in Nineveh and the Babylonians in Babylon. It was generally accepted that all diseases were caused by demons and sent by gods to punish men. Their physician-priests were trained in the best methods of exorcising the demons which consisted of prayers, incantations, and ritual performances. Astrology was also important. On the other hand, the Code of Hammurabi, written about

2000 B.C., prescribed mineral and herbal cures and recommended magic only to please the patient.

**India.** In India, the oldest and most sacred of Hindu books of knowledge, the Vedas, contains the earliest classification of mental derangements and traces their origins to angry gods and devils. Unfortunately, the Hindu beliefs in reincarnation and transmigration of souls, coupled with their association of theology with psychical phenomena stifled the development of psychological theory. To them all suffering in this life was punishment for crimes committed in a previous life and was acceptable in the present because of the hope that the next life would be better. They also believed that ignorance was in the abdomen, passion in the chest, and goodness in the brain. A great Hindu physician, Susruta, was one of the earliest to suggest that strong passion could cause not only mental but physical disease, the most important principle of psychosomatic medicine. Buddha, a Hindu prince (563–483 B.C.), taught introspection and meditation as a means of reaching a state of tranquility. The great religion named after him has helped millions through the centuries in both Eastern and Western cultures, by means of contemplative techniques, to deal with life's emotional difficulties.

**China.** In ancient China, the Yellow Emperor who lived a hundred years, from 2698 to 2598 B.C., wrote that anxiety was similar to a disease, and that fear, apprehension, and agitation can cause changes in the body and mind. His medical book, the *Nei Ching*, stressed the importance of inner conflicts leading to disease. Two thousand years later Confucius, who lived in the fifth century B.C., stressed veneration of the father, family, and ancestors, and high moral conduct. This led to family closeness and security which lessened vulnerability to emotional illness. As early as 1140 B.C. there were mental institutions of sorts in China, and almshouses for the mentally deranged were certainly in existence there by the third century B.C.

**The Hebrews.** The Hebrews had the concept of one God who was righteous and perfect. Illness in any form was regarded as judgment and part of God's will. Any other view was blasphemy. For example, King Saul's mental illness is described in 1 Samuel 16:14 "But the Spirit of the Lord departed from Saul, and an evil spirit from the Lord troubled him." Since God had sent the illness, no human means could remove it; salvation, not treatment, was needed. Only prayer to God for forgiveness or appeal to one of His prophets could sometimes bring a cure. Since the heart was regarded as the center of the intellect and emotions, one of the duties of a prophet of the Lord was "to bind up the brokenhearted" (Isaiah 61:1). For these reasons there were no medical texts of methods of treatment, but the Scriptures contain many accounts of mental disease.

*Old Testament examples.* Saul's extremes of bizarre behavior were probably due to manic-depressive illness. His delusion that David was plotting against him was paranoia and his suicide the end result of hopelessness and reactive depression. David pretended to be mad when he was among the Philistines (1 Samuel 21:14–15), a good example of malingering. The falling disease often described in the Old Testament was probably epilepsy. Nebuchadnezzar, King of Babylon, as described in Daniel 4:-31–34 ended his days as a psychotic with the delusion that he had turned into a wolf. The law in Leviticus 20:27 that him with a "familiar spirit, or that is a wizard" should be executed was carried over for centuries as justification for persecution of the mentally ill. Later Hebrew writings, however, such as the Talmud, recommended protection and justice for the mentally ill. It also was prepared to understand and forgive the suicide, an attitude very different from the fear and hostility expressed by surrounding nations at that time.

**Ancient Greeks.** The ancient Greeks also believed that insanity was a punishment from offended gods. This is found in

Homer's hexametric poems written about 1000 B.C. At the time when the cult of Asklepios (Latin: Aesculapius) dominated Greek medicine, to its temples of healing patients flocked for therapy consisting of ritual, religion, dream therapy, hypnotic drugs, and sunbathing. Later, however, during the Golden Age great philosophers such as Socrates (469–399 B.C.) became unsatisfied with accepting the supernatural and sought rational explanations for the mysteries of life. This represented a great breakthrough and was the true beginning of our present scientific era. Alcmaeon of Crotona (c. 500 B.C.), a pupil of Pythagoras (c. 530 B.C.), dissected and taught that the brain secreted thought. Hippocrates (460–375 B.C.) also recognized the brain as the distribution center for intelligence and feeling though he believed that air was the vital element it distributed.

*The period of the great philosophers.* Empedocles (490–430 B.C.) taught that the earth consisted of the four elements, earth, air, fire, and water, with the four qualities, cold, dry, hot, and moist. He also first pointed out that love and hate had an influence on changing human behavior.

Plato (427–347 B.C.) taught that the mind and body were controlled by the tripartite soul: reason in the brain, emotion in the chest, and appetite in the abdomen. Aristotle (384–322 B.C.), however, believed that the heart was the center of thought and the brain merely cooled the hot vapors rising from the heart, thereby preventing intemperance.

Hippocrates incorporated the principles of Empedocles to apply to man who contained four humors: blood, hot and moist; yellow bile, hot and dry; black bile, cold and dry; and phlegm, cold and moist. A man's mental qualities and emotional state depended on the relative proportions of these. He described such personality types as sanguine, choleric, melancholic, and phlegmatic derived from these humors and said that too much black bile (melancholia) caused depression. He also first described with great clinical accuracy such conditions as epilepsy, mania, postpartum psychosis, paranoia, acute brain syndrome, and hysteria. He firmly denied gods as causative agents in disease. Such was his great reputation that if he said a criminal was suffering from paranoia the court would commute his sentence from execution to imprisonment. Asclepiades (first century B.C.), first classified insanity into acute and chronic conditions and taught the connection between the emotions and the mind. He prescribed rocking chairs, hot baths, massages, and music therapy for his patients and kept them in well-lighted places.

*Palestine in Christ's day.* In the time of Christ Greek and Roman influence in Palestine brought medical science there to a level equivalent to their countries of origin. The Jews, however, still had the ancient idea that all illness was a sign of God's displeasure. Many times when Jesus healed sick people He associated His act with forgiveness. He also stressed the element of faith on the part of the patient as a necessary prerequisite for the miracle to be effective. Faith in the doctor today still helps patients to get well again more quickly. The Gospels repeatedly stress that many more healing miracles were performed by Christ than the few actually recorded. The Christian era ever since has seen a continuing onslaught on the related forces of evil and disease. Hence the fact that the vast majority of hospitals in Christendom in the Middle Ages were started and run by Christian monks and nuns. Up to about two hundred years ago, before the medical profession had achieved the social and intellectual status it now enjoys, the strongest motivation in becoming a physician was the Christian doctrine of loving one's neighbor.

**Rome.**    Six hundred years after Hippocrates, the great Greek physician Galen (A.D. 130–200) who was practicing in Rome still used his theories but greatly elaborated on them. He said the brain and not the heart was the seat of the soul. Aretaeus (c. A.D.100) another Roman physician was the first to observe and describe mentally ill patients on whom he did thorough follow-up studies. He was the first to notice that manic and depressive states could exist in the same person with normal intervals between. He emphasized that mental illness was not necessarily accompanied by intellectual deterioration. Cicero (106–43B.C.), though not a physician, wrote that bodily ailments could result from emotional turmoil. Celsus in his *De re medica* described many neuro-psychiatric conditions and Soranus described phrenitis, a disease of the mind, from which we derive our word frenzy. He stressed humane treatment of the mentally deranged and that restraints should be used only as a last resort.

**Influence of the Arabian Empire.**    After the barbarians destroyed Rome in the fifth century, the Dark Ages settled over Europe for a thousand years and very little intellectual progress was made. However, during this period the great Moslem Arabian Empire of North Africa and the Near East played a vital role in the preservation and development of medical and scientific knowledge. Rhazes (865–923) was head of a large hospital in Baghdad. He was famous as a bedside clinician, and he used a primitive form of psychotherapy on those he recognized to be mentally ill. Avicenna (980–1037), born in Persia, wrote the *Canon of Medicine,* a summary of all medical knowledge up to that time. For the next six hundred years it supplanted Galen's works, which had been medicine's "bible" since the second century. In the *Canon* Avicenna gives an extensive classification of mental disorders, and being free from the medieval Christian theories of demons, he was able to make clear-cut clinical descriptions of them. The major contributions of the Arabs were the greatly increased number of drugs and medicines they used and the numerous hospitals they founded all over the empire from Spain to the borders of India.

*Maimonides.* One of the greatest physicians was Maimonides (1135–1204), the Jewish humanist who taught that religious faith and scientific explorations need not be incompatible. He wrote a code of medical ethics, updating the Hippocratic Oath, which is still valid today. He stressed treatment of the patient as a whole, not just his disease, and emphasized that a morally upright life contributed to mental health.

**Demonology and the witches.** When the Tartars took and destroyed Baghdad in the thirteenth century, and the rising power of the Turks weakened Arabia's military might, much of the glorious culture of Islam's golden age disappeared. Demonology was rampant in Christian Europe and the Church a decadent political despot. Belief in witchcraft then reached its peak and became a Church-sponsored universal obsession. The devil was represented by demons who entered into people's minds and made them crazy. Psychotic, unmarried older women in particular were singled out as having signed a pact with the devil, and it was the Christian's duty to destroy them. Eventually all witches were branded as heretics, and it was decreed that insanity was a sign of infidelity to the true faith of the Church. Thousands of psychotic women were burned at the stake as witches, their executioners believing that it was actually an act of mercy since the purging by fire would cleanse their souls for heaven.

*Johann Weyer.* Horrified by these inhuman acts, the Dutch physician Johann Weyer thoroughly investigated every witch-hunt brought to his attention over a twelve-year period including a clinical interview of the accused before execution. Then in 1563 he published a book stating that most witches were really mentally ill people needing not ecclesiastical judgment but a physician. Because he separated medical psychology from theology and gave detailed descriptions of psychiatric disturbances, he has been called the founder of modern psychiatry.

**Early mental hospitals.**    In the days following the witches, mentally ill people continued to be feared and rejected by society, which often hounded them from one town to the next. A few were accepted into monasteries, nunneries, almshouses, and primitive asylums. London's Bethlehem Royal Hospital (Bedlam) began accepting the insane as patients in 1377, but their treatment was appalling with filthy conditions, poor food, cruel restrictions, dark cells, brutal attendants, and public viewing days. On these occasions, for a penny, people could gape at them and be entertained by the antics of the lunatics.

**Eighteenth-century Europe more humane.**    In the seventeenth century Sir Francis Bacon and other philosophers began to teach that there was a connection between the functions of the mind and the natural order in the universe. As a result, toward the end of the eighteenth century more humane treatment began to be practiced. In Italy Chiarurgi (1739–1820) was the one most responsible for the change. In Germany rationality was the influence behind the change. In England it was the religious revival under the preaching of Wesley and Whitfield. There, William Tuke, a member of the Quaker Society of Friends, opened in 1796 The Retreat in York, a place for the mentally ill. It was humanely run years in advance of its time. In France, Philippe Pinel (1745–1826), when physician-in-chief at the Bicêtre Hospital in Paris, ordered all chains removed from inmates, and he instituted there, and at the Salpêtrière, a new type of "moral treatment."

**Conditions in America.**    *Benjamin Rush.*    In America treatment of the mentally ill was essentially the same as in Europe. In colonial days witches were hanged or drowned in ducking stools, and insane people thrown into prison. The Pennsylvania Hospital in Philadelphia, established in 1752, was the first general hospital in America and the first to accept mental patients. Benjamin Rush, the father of American psychiatry, was on the staff there and stimulated interest in the possibility of treating mental illness. He stressed that it was not hopeless, and he insisted on hygienic conditions.

**Development of psychiatry.** *Jackson, Mesmer, Charcot, and Kraepelin.* Increase in available mental hospitals in the eighteenth and nineteenth centuries led to the development of clinical psychiatry. Study of how causes lead to effects in mental illness (psychodynamics) was given a great boost in this period by the great English neurologist John Hughlings Jackson and by the evolutionary theory of Charles Darwin. Meanwhile, the rediscovery of "animal magnetism" or hypnotism by Franz Anton Mesmer (1734–1815), and its practical use by James Braid (1795–1860) in England and Jean Martin Charcot (1825–93) in Paris in investigating causes of mental diseases, led to the development of modern principles of psychotherapy. Charcot, like Mesmer, used hypnotism to cure hysteria and started serious medical investigations into it and other phenomena. At about the same time Emil Kraepelin (1856–1926) in Germany systematized a thoroughly comprehensive description of all mental diseases. He distinguished between a disease category itself and the symptoms the disease produced. His work paved the way for the establishment of psychiatry as a medical science.

*Sigmund Freud.* One of Charcot's students, Sigmund Freud (1856–1939), practiced as a neurologist in Vienna and used hypnotism to investigate neurotic symptoms. He developed the free association technique of analyzing patients whom he told to speak aloud whatever came into their minds. This later evolved into the technique of psychoanalysis. Freud described for the first time the concept of the unconscious mind influencing thought, emotions, and behavior. By bringing unconscious material into conscious awareness, patients' symptoms were sometimes relieved. His theory of infantile sexuality and libido development, and his concept of the id, ego, and superego were two other significant contributions to present day psychiatric practice. He was the first to use the couch in his technique of analyzing patients, and more than anyone else he popularized psychotherapy as it is now practiced.

# 2
# THE PSYCHOLOGICAL VALUE
# OF A PERSONAL CHRISTIAN FAITH

**Both divine and human help needed.**     In chapter 1, I made
the point that we believing Christians are just as susceptible to
mental illness as non-Christians. When we become ill we need
help both human and divine. We need medical attention, but we
also have available a personal faith in God's power which can heal
our sick bodies and minds. But is it God's power alone that heals
or our own faith in that power? From my personal experience,
both as a physician and as a patient, having undergone nine
operations, I testify that it is both. Sir William Osler, famous
nineteenth century physician, said, "I treat, God heals." Without
God's continuing providential care the human race would never
have survived beyond the Garden of Eden, but in addition all
experienced physicians would agree that the patient's attitude
toward his physical sickness is a key factor in successful recovery.
The resentful, fearful, or depressed patient takes a long time to
heal, whereas the one who has trust, assurance, optimism, and an
ability to accept his situation with patience heals relatively more
quickly. These same qualities are also of value in reducing the
severity of certain emotional disorders or even sometimes preventing them altogether. The devout Christian has these qualities, or at least has access to them through his personal faith.
Only his unconfessed resentment can block his receiving them as
God's healing gift.

**Doubt.**     At this point something must be said about doubt. I have been criticized for avoiding difficult problems in this whole subject by simply making dogmatic assertions based on my own credo without facing the tensions and doubts others experience in their own quests after truth. These criticisms are partly true. Millions would like to find peace with God but have failed to find it by searching. I understand their struggles. I was not raised as a Christian. I never even went to church as a child, let alone Sunday school. I had to attend compulsory chapel when I was at a prep school in England and got about as much from it as most other boys: I heard the basic facts of the Christian gospel and acquired a superficial knowledge of Biblical history. The thought that Jesus Christ was a spiritual being alive today with a claim on my allegiance never occurred to me. Religion was an institution, not something personal. I was already a young adult, a student at Cambridge University, when I first realized that the Christian faith was something I could become personally involved in and that Jesus Christ offered Himself to me as my own Saviour and Lord.

*Personal testimony.*     My conversion was by no means a sudden emotional affair. It took many months of struggle within myself. I felt like a little pawn in a huge game, a conflict between the devil and the Holy Spirit. Cambridge, immediately after World War II, was a seething arena of new ideas contesting with each other for the opportunity of making a better world. We had as a nation prayed for victory while the bombs were falling on London, but when that was over so were the Thanksgiving services, and God was forgotten.

"Come now, as a student of the natural sciences how can you possibly believe in the virgin birth of Christ? Do you honestly believe in the resurrection as a historic fact?" Most of my good friends felt sorry for me and ridiculed my attempts to make sense of the challenging concepts I was exploring. Although I had just finished eighteen months in the army before going to Cambridge, many of my classmates had been through the war and were a few years older than I was. I respected their experience and maturity, but this very fact made their scepticism harder for me to cope with. They forced me to think. They forced me to pray for spiritual illumination and think again. They forced me to study the Scriptures, and think again. My searching was so intensive that I failed some of my exams the first time and would have been expelled if I had not passed them at the second attempt. Gradually, however, some sort of light glimmered and with it came a willingness to step out in faith. Yes, I had doubts, plenty of them, and I still have. I would be grossly dishonest not to admit that I still have many doubts, some of which will only be dispelled when I stand in my own glorified resurrection body before the throne of my God. I respect and sympathize with those today who have doubts and are struggling, as I am still, to grow in understanding and faith. I know how they feel. I have been through it myself.

*Direction, not distance, important.*   We are all traveling along the road of life. I do not think that God cares very much how far along that road we have gone, but He *does* care about the direction in which we are going. It is a matter of the will in the ultimate analysis. The right direction is the act of the will in which we desire to progress toward deeper communion with God and unselfish service to our fellowman. I have come a short distance along that road. I have a long way to go, but I must not look back. While respecting other's doubts, therefore, and also admitting my own, I must nevertheless stand fast at the point along the road that I have reached and progress from there.

**Factors affecting mental health in Christians.**     Specifically, then, for those of us who consider ourselves Christian believers, what are the factors in our lives that are different from our pre-conversion days and which now contribute toward our mental health and emotional stability? I think these factors are forgiveness, security, guidance, fellowship, identity, and structure.

*Forgiveness.* Guilt is one of the commonest symptoms I see in my office every day because it is often the root cause of either the anxiety or depression which first brought the patient to me. For the Christian, guilt feelings lead to separation from God and fear of condemnation. His spiritual communion with Christ is broken by sin and he experiences guilt, true or false. (The distinction is explained in chapter 9.) Confession and repentance lead to assurance of forgiveness by God and a restoration of that communion. For the Catholic, ritualized confession to a priest obtains absolution from him. The evangelical Christian has to accept by faith absolution direct from God. In both cases confession has to be accompanied by genuine inner repentance and change of heart. If it is not, it is merely an attempt to avoid guilt feelings by deluding oneself that the mere admission of sin by itself is all that is needed. With *real repentance,* however, the burden of separation from God is lifted and the feelings of guilt disappear. This brings an overwhelming sense of relief and peace of mind. Anxiety is calmed and depression is lifted. When I first became a believing Christian, the most dramatic thing I noticed was the tranquilizing and antidepressant effect that my newfound peace with God gave me. This peace, as I understand it, was the emotional counterpart of the intellectual knowledge of forgiveness. Intellectually I knew I had been justified by faith, but emotionally that knowledge was sealed by the disappearance of tension and depressed mood. Nor was this experience only temporary for me. In the twenty years that have passed since then the daily obtaining of forgiveness for sins recently committed has preserved a close walk with Christ which constantly maintains my inner peace.

*Security.*  Assurance of forgiveness leads to assurance of salvation. The hope of the church is the certainty of the second coming of Christ and the hope of the individual Christian is the certainty of spending eternity in the presence of his Saviour. But there is another hope, another certainty so often overlooked by fearful Christians weak in faith. This is the hope for today in *this* life and the certainty that watching over him is God's providential care. Even though suffering and tragedy may come, the strong believer knows that "all things work together for good to them that love God, to them who are the called according to his purpose" (Romans 8:28). Incomplete understanding of that purpose in this life does not detract from the Christian's ability to accept that what is happening to him *is* part of God's loving eternal plan for him. If he can say, "Though he slay me, yet will I trust in him" (Job 13:15), he has that quality of tranquility that contributes immeasurably to the healing of body and mind, or to acceptance if approaching death. This security of knowing that his daily life is in God's care calms many anxious fears and reduces the apprehensions of the unknown. Such faith relaxes inner tensions and removes many worries which can make us physically ill. The heavy burdens of sadness, mourning, and depression are lifted by the security we feel in the assurance of a brighter future.

*Guidance.*  The next step, after the establishment of assurance of forgiveness and security in this life, is the practical issue of the responsibilities of daily Christian living. What does a Christian really mean when he says he lives for Christ or when he claims that he is in the center of God's will for his life? How can he be sure? How does he actually obtain guidance from God?

We are entering now into the very core of the psychological factors that are involved in man's relationship with God. We are treading on delicate ground: the transitional territory between the mind and the soul, the psychological and the spiritual. It is the area where science and religion touch, the area of evidence and experience rather than proof. It is the down-to-earth issue of what personal religion is really all about at the level of real communication between man and God.

*How God and man communicate.* The third person of the Trinity is a person, not an "it." He has a power, sometimes called the power of the Holy Spirit. But He is a person with a personality and a personal influence. He is capable of interpersonal relationships with men. It is He who is God's means of direct communication with the mind of man. It is with the mind in the cerebral cortex that man's brain thinks, calculates, remembers, and with which man formulates words both for human communication and prayer. Here is his psyche, his conscious awareness. Here is the most highly developed part of his brain. If you believe in evolution, this is the most recent development not present to this degree in lower animals. If you believe in special creation, this is the significant difference between Adam and Eve and all previous animal creation. It was with the mind that our first parents were able to communicate with God: it is through our minds today that the person of the Holy Spirit communicates with us.

Notice I stress *mind:* this has nothing to do with *will* or *emotions.* These are influenced by the mind after the Holy Spirit has influenced it. This sequence is most important in order to avoid error. Dr. D. Martyn Lloyd-Jones in his book *Conversions Psychological and Spiritual* states:

> Another important principle is that in presenting the Christian gospel we must never, in the first place, make a direct approach either to the emotions or to the will. The emotions and the will should always be influenced through the mind. Truth is intended to come to the mind. The normal course is for the emotions and the

will to be affected by the truth after it has first entered and gripped the mind. It seems to me that this is a principle of Holy Scripture. The approach to the emotions and the will should be indirect. Still less should we ever bring any pressure to bear upon either the emotions or the will. We are to "plead" with men but never to bring pressure. We are to "beseech," but we are never to browbeat. This, it seems to me, is a vital distinction which every preacher and missioner must always bear in mind.

Now, precisely how does the Holy Spirit impart truth to the believer? It is too simple to say just *prayer* though this is partly the answer. What really is prayer in my experience? Prayer for me is thinking: an intense mental striving, an extreme form of cerebral exercise. Will and emotions are involved but only secondarily. I think; I use words; I express my thoughts partly to myself, partly directed toward God. Nothing happens. I am reminded by the Holy Spirit that there is some unrepented sin creating a block. I change gears and talk with God about sin, admitting it and asking for the ability to repent. Sometimes immediately, sometimes not for a long time, I become willing to repent, and do so. The will and emotions are being involved. Fellowship is restored. Now back to the original issue. I think about it again and gradually fresh thoughts come into my mind: a decision to be made, a course of action to be taken. I think about the alternatives and ask God to influence my will and emotions to make the correct choice. I desire that my decision should be in conformity with God's plan for my life and for the lives of others, and I trust Him to guide me in making the right one. I am reminded of His words to Isaiah: "And thine ears shall hear a word behind thee, saying, This is the way, walk ye in it,

when ye turn to the right hand, and when ye turn to the left"
(Isaiah 30:21).

If my decision is in fact God's will for me, He gives me peace
of mind and the inner conviction that I did the right thing. If,
however, I have made a mistake, I have to trust God that as soon
as possible He will show me my error and give me the wisdom
and strength to change my decision to the correct one. It is when
Christians do not do this that they drift into error, and it is when
they are unwilling to admit their error that sin is committed. It
is the will and emotions again usurping the ruling authority of the
mind. In the final analysis this is just what sin is: will and emotions
rebelling against the influence of God in the mind. This is why
two Christians can come to two opposite conclusions about an
issue. One or both of them has permitted the will or emotions to
take precedence over the Spirit-controlled mind.

In addition to prayer, however, there are some other practical
ways in which God influences our decisions and thereby guides
our lives. Regular *systematic Bible study* and personal searching of
the Scriptures is the most important way in which we soak our
minds with the principles of the Word of God. It becomes
progressively easier for us to recognize the influence of the Holy
Spirit on our minds if we are prepared by deeper and deeper
understanding of the contents of both the Old and New Testaments. A misuse of Scripture is to think that a particular verse
dug out of context is the absolute answer to a particular problem.
This can happen rarely. Usually it is the diligent study of God's
Word over months and years that gives the mind the ingredients
with which Spirit-guided decisions can be correctly made.
Remember that the Spirit *never* guides us contrary to the basic
teachings of the Bible. When in doubt test Scripture with Scripture. Compare and contrast different verses which seem to apply
to the issue to be decided. Use your God-given brain and think,

really deeply think about the problems to be solved. Shallow thinking is the worst enemy of the Christian desiring God's will in his life, because this is powerless to maintain the mind's necessary dominance over the will and emotions.

*Fellowship.*  When an individual has made a personal commitment to Jesus Christ as his personal Saviour and Lord, he suddenly finds that he has something in common with many other people. Frequently he finds that this common commitment enables him to develop deep, lasting friendships with a wide variety of different sorts of people with whom he had previously had very little in common. He may unexpectedly discover, for example, that a new friendship with someone he has just met who has a similar faith, is much more meaningful to him than a friendship he has had for many years with someone else without this faith. The mutually protective comradeship of football players on the field or of combat troops in action against the enemy is surprisingly similar in some ways to the fellowship of Christians. There is a common leader, a common adversary, a common objective, and a common plan to achieve it. Christ is the leader, sin the adversary, restoration of the world to communion with God the objective, and preaching the gospel and providing fellowship for converts the plan.

Christian fellowship in a church, or in another group such as a Bible study union in college, is not only helpful but essential for the development of personal spiritual maturity in the growing believer. It is also a group of people where strangers find acceptance. The downtrodden and rejected by society often gravitate to a church where they at least feel that some attempt is being made to understand and help them. This is often the reason why some churches have some peculiar people in them. The mentally defective, the severe neurotic, the schizophrenic, and the psychopath find often in a local church a group of people who try to befriend them and support them where possible. In addition, the not-so-sick people with personality disorders or adjustment problems also find churches places where they can more easily make friends than in the cold, rejecting world outside. Healthy sceptics who then come to visit and evaluate should by every means possible be persuaded not to judge the Christian faith by the sick people he meets in church. The Christian faith must be judged on its own merits, not by the peculiarities of some of its adherents. Speaking more positively, the particular quality of good Christian fellowship is love: love by strangers for each other made possible by the spiritual nature of their relationship.

*Identity.*   Every person is a unique individual. Even identical twins have many points of difference. No one has exactly the same face, body, mind, or personality as anyone else. Yet, in the present time, especially in the pressure cookers of modern urban living, there is a tendency to feel other than uinque. We cram ourselves into commuter trains and wonder if we are just little cogs in a big machine. How insignificant I feel when I think of the fact that there are eight million other people in New York and that I am only one of over three billion souls on earth. Young people in particular feel very sensitive about their identities as individual persons, partly because the younger one is the less time one has had to develop a distinctive personality. The lack of a sense of personal identity is a major contributing factor in many of the emotional problems of youth.

There is a difference, however, for the Christian for at least three reasons. First, he knows that he has an individual relationship with his Creator and Redeemer, a relationship which is renewed and kept fresh by his personal daily devotions. Second, he is a member of a loving and accepting fellowship, the church. He matters to it, too. He is a vital part of the body of Christ, of the bride adorned for the heavenly Bridegroom. What he does affects others. What they do affects him. Third, he has a definite purpose in life. Both on an individual and communal level, he is living and working for the glory of God and for the furtherance of the Kingdom of Christ in that part of the world where God has called him.

As a psychiatrist I have seen many people who are depressed and who have lost hope and faith in themselves. Probably the most abject misery I have ever witnessed, however, has been in the lives of _backsliding Christians_, who once experienced the joy of fellowship with Christ and His church but who now for one reason or another have forsaken their former identification with it. They preserve a brave front and try to kid themselves and others that they are now happier, freed from the limitations of a Christian style of living. But it does not take very long for a psychiatrist, or anyone else for that matter, to discover that deep down inside there is a terrible void. They feel unfulfilled, rejected, unworthy, and incapable of being satisfied with all that they have tried to substitute for the life of faith.

*Structure.*   Not only Christianity, but any religion, can help provide for a race or nation a unifying force. In a certain sense this type of structure on a national level can be useful but there is also a danger. In America today it is very important that we do not permit in our thinking the concept that the middle-class Establishment, which we claim made this country as great as it is, is somehow the special object of God's blessing and favor. We Protestants are very prone to believe that because most born-again Christians, so we think, are like us, God must therefore have a very special place for us in His great plan. He has indeed got a special purpose for us, but only on the basis of obedience to His commandments will He continue to shower us with so many material blessings. Ancient Israel was very much the object of His favor until national disobedience to His statutes resulted in total destruction by a pagan enemy. God will indeed continue to bless us as a nation if we turn in repentance to Him. If we do not, we will share the same fate as the Roman Empire.

The structure which a national religion can provide is seen more clearly in the context of the basic unit, *the family*. Specifically, a Christian family, in which both parents are believers and in which the children are raised to be followers of Christ, has in its makeup a system of beliefs and moral principles to guide their standards of behavior. A family which basically believes in the Christian teachings has a base line from which all members can deduce the ethical standards expected of them. Their religious and moral principles form a guide for all decisions that have to be made. A well-recognized and honestly practiced family faith provides each developing child with a structure of his own with which he can later learn to make his own decisions.

On an individual level the fact that I know the teachings of Christ guides me to live my whole life within those tenets. The New Testament does not give all the particular do's and don't of every present-day decision I have to make, but in spite of being almost two thousand years old, it does give me all the basic information I need to ensure that I make them within the limits of the perfect standards of God's holiness. The power of the Holy Spirit, of course, is provided to help me to live to this high standard so long as my will permits it.

# 3
# MENTAL HEALTH AND HOW
# TO KEEP IT

**Christians can become mentally ill.**   We Christians sometimes have great difficulty in admitting what is happening to
ourselves or our loved ones when we become mentally ill. We
assume that because we are now possessed by the Holy Spirit
somehow this magically protects us from psychological or emotional problems. In fact, however, this is no more the case than
that being a Christian protects us from getting mumps or
measles. One of the reasons we deny evidence of illness is because we are simply ignorant of the signs and symptoms of mental illnesses.

*Normal to be a little abnormal.*   Before describing mental illness,
however, some attempt will be made to define mental health.
This is difficult and probably no one person's description would
be complete. Many things would have to be considered as characteristics of mental health but not all of them would be present in
any one individual. In other words, everyone has certain little
personal foibles which someone else might regard as abnormal.
How true is the old Welsh saying: "All the world is queer save
thee and me, and even thee's a little queer"! This essentially
means that it is quite normal to be a little bit abnormal. In the
Christian context remember that normality does not mean sinless
perfection. Only three people in all of human history were completely healthy, normal, and sinless: Adam and Eve before the
Fall and Jesus Christ. The first two were expelled from Eden by

a Holy God for disobedience, and thereafter they and their progeny became subject to physiological and psychological pathology, leading eventually to death. The latter was murdered by sinful men precisely because His perfect standards were too much of a threat to them. With these exceptions, too much normality would make an individual very dull. It is the unusual characteristics of man, those facets of his personality which make him abnormal, which make him a unique and interesting person, even if some others think he is "a little queer." Many of the great leaders of history have been men with significant personal abnormalities.

*Functional abnormality the clue to sickness.* The normalcy of abnormality is generally acceptable, within reason, in personality structure; but not in functioning. It is here, in the evaluation of how a person functions, that one is confronted with the distinction between health and illness. In studying cardiology we are taught that if the heart has a murmur when heard through a stethoscope it probably is of no significance if the heart functions properly in its duty of circulating the blood. But if the murmur is associated with a failure of function, then treatment is indicated. Likewise, if a peculiarity in personality structure is related to abnormal functioning in daily life, something should be done about it.

**Characteristics of mental health.** In order to avoid the complication of cultural differences, the following suggested characteristics of mental health are considered in the context of a man or woman functioning in his or her own familiar environment and culture. (1) In general terms the mentally healthy person must be in contact with reality and prove this by behaving and reacting to all situations in a realistic way. (2) This means that he should be able to function successfully in the major experiences of life, that is, in his vocational and social life, and in his personal and sexual life. "Successfully" should be understood as meaning a quality of functioning which is appropriate and satisfactory both to himself and to other people directly or indirectly involved. Specifically, then, successful functioning would normally consist of the healthy person performing well in his job (or at school if he is still in training), having some friends and the ability to make and keep friends, being able to enjoy healthy social or sporting activities, and being able to love and be loved either by being happily married or well adjusted in his intimate interpersonal relationships. (3) When something goes wrong in any of these areas, it is an important characteristic of the mentally healthy person that he adapts and adjusts to the changed situation with self-control and discipline. His reaction to the disappointment, worry, or stress in any form will be to deal with it in an unselfish and yet self-confident manner. He should be free from excessive anxiety or depression. Sublimation or some form of redirection of energy is often an appropriate way of dealing with certain pressures or temptations. (4) Whatever the course of action is, it should not be either self-destructive or harmful in any way to others. All effective functioning should be within the confines of strong stable emotional control and the acceptance of responsibility for one's actions. (5) Also, the healthy person will usually have worthwhile goals in life that he is seeking to achieve within the rules of the society in which he lives. However small or great his personal ambitions may be, his striving through the battles of life should provide him with a sense of purpose and lead him to some measure of satisfaction, contentment, happiness, and inner peace.

**Spiritual dimension also needed.**     For the committed Christian there is an additional dimension. To him God is the ultimate reality, and spiritual and psychological health is to be in contact with that reality. Personal encounters for the Christian are in three directions: inward toward the self, outward toward others, and upward toward God. Total health in the whole man demands healthy relationships in all three areas. Also health in body, mind, and spirit is a total concept. If any one part is sick, the whole man is affected. For the Christian complete health in the whole man must, therefore, necessarily include a right personal relationship with Jesus Christ as Saviour and Lord. The non-Christian may not have this spiritual dimension, but even without it he may be better off in terms of interhuman functioning than the Christian in whom the spiritual part of life is separated from Christ. (See chapter 5.) The worst situation of all is the case of the Christian who professes a nominal allegiance to Christ but who is in fact separated from Him by sin. Examples of this form of mental and spiritual illness are manifest throughout human history in the "Holy" wars, the Inquisition, the burning of "heretics" by both Catholics and Protestants, the inhuman treatment of the mentally ill, and the murder of six million Jews by one of the most highly civilized "Christian" nations in the world.

*Health, the fruit of the Spirit.*   The true Christian, however, is able to demonstrate his total health by the quality of his life. His belief in the divine inspiration of Scripture helps him to become "perfectly fit and thoroughly equipped for every good enterprise" (2 Timothy 3:17 WILLIAMS). The good enterprises he is exhorted to pursue are summed up by Paul in his letter to the Galatians describing the results of being filled by the Holy Spirit: "The Spirit, however, produces in human life fruits such as these: love, joy, peace, patience, kindness, generosity, fidelity, tolerance and self-control" (Galatians 5:22–23 PHILLIPS). Christian moral character and mental health are manifested by these graces and are made possible in the believer because of his vital union with Christ.

**Principles for maintaining mental health.**   Assuming he has it in the first place, the Christian can maintain his mental health, and avoid significant neurotic problems, for example, by observing some of these principles throughout life: (1) He should accept the fact that life is not a bed of roses. There will be difficulties and disappointments to which he must continuously be prepared to adjust himself. This accepting attitude and ability to adjust is made easier for him by his assurance of the overruling providence of a loving God. (2) He should be willing at all times to react to other people in a humble and loving way and to be unselfish and forgiving in all his relationships. (3) He should develop for himself a place in life wherein he can feel secure and function successfully within the limits of his abilities. It is essential that he have always before him some goal he is striving to achieve, and when one is reached to his satisfaction, he must strive for the next. (4) He *must* have something to look forward to. All work and no play makes Jack a dull boy. Christians especially fail in this area. So many seem to believe it is a sin to enjoy themselves, forgetting the exhortation to Timothy that we should trust God "who giveth us richly all things to enjoy" (1 Timothy 6:17). There are thousands of wholesome ways in which Christians, young and old, can find pleasure and happiness in this life, without guilt feelings or fear that they might be incurring God's disapproval. (5) Finally, there is no doubt that a strong personal faith which encompasses a profound belief and trust in God and a willingness to be led by the Holy Spirit in positive activity can contribute significantly to the Christian's ability to accept or adjust to the pressures of life which might otherwise threaten his emotional stability and mental health. Wholeness of faith consists of belief and trust leading to practical action. All three are necessary for total health in the Christian.

# 4
# MENTAL ILLNESS: THE PSYCHOSES

**Differences between psychosis and neurosis.**    True mental illnesses, the psychotic conditions, are differentiated from the neurotic conditions in the following ways: A psychosis is a severe disorder of psychological functioning manifested by a loss of contact with reality. A neurosis is a disorder in which reality testing remains relatively intact but internal conflicts give rise to such symptoms as anxiety, depression, obsessions, unreasonable fears or doubts, and certain physical ills of psychogenic origin. A psychotic often experiences perceptual disruptions such as delusions or hallucinations; that is, he may believe something which is not true, or he may hear voices or see things which are not really there. Much of his time is spent in a world of fantasy. His mental functioning is sometimes so impaired that it grossly interferes with his capacity to meet the ordinary demands of daily living. Mood, memory, and clear logical thinking are sometimes so severely affected that he becomes unable to take care of himself or behave appropriately in the company of others. At this stage, for mutual protection, compulsory hospitalization becomes mandatory. By contrast the neurotic is capable of normal daily activities even though he feels very uncomfortable inside. He does not suffer the psychotic's agony of acute mental confusion which is obvious to all, but rather he suffers the unpleasant symptoms already mentioned which he struggles to keep bottled up inside himself for fear of being thought by others to be crazy. The psychotic is incapable of conscious control of his condition since he has lost insight, whereas the neurotic does retain a variable degree of control over his symptoms since insight is not as much affected.

*Differences in treatment.* Psychotics need hospitalization, major tranquilizers, supportive psychotherapy, and sometimes electroconvulsive shock treatment. Neurotics need directive or nondirective psychotherapy, minor tranquilizers or antidepressant medications, and can usually be treated successfully as outpatients. The causes of the psychoses vary from organic brain disease to some generalized internal chemical imbalance in the body systems. The chemical causes of the neuroses are unknown in the present state of medical knowledge, but there is no shortage of theories of possible psychological or spiritual causes. (See chapter 8.)

**Organic brain diseases.** The psychoses are classified in two major categories, the organic and the functional. Organic brain syndromes causing psychoses are the result of some actual physical or chemical damage to the brain matter itself. The commonest causes of temporary brain dysfunction are excessive alcohol and drugs, but these last for only a few hours or less until the body has excreted the offending substance. The symptoms pass away but certainly some permanent damage has been caused, even if only minimally. Other poisons such as arsenic, lead, or mercury compounds can cause longer lasting effects. So can infections such as syphilis and virus encephalitis, and various conditions such as meningitis and brain abscess caused by bacteria. Intermittent symptoms can be associated with epilepsy. General physical illnesses can also cause organic brain diseases. These include malnutrition; various endocrine gland problems such as diabetes, thyroid, pituitary, and adrenal disorders; and certain fevers such as malaria, pneumonia, typhoid, and acute rheumatic fever. A severe head injury can cause both psychiatric symptoms and loss of intellectual ability. Permanent damage is seen in cancer or tumor of the brain, in a stroke or brain hemorrhage, and in cerebral arteriosclerosis or hardening of the arteries, sometimes called senile dementia, caused by poor blood circulation to the brain. Typical symptoms of senile organic brain disease include slowing down of thinking processes, confusion of thought, failing memory, emotional lability with spontaneous bouts of inappropriate weeping, laughter, anger, or impatience, and disorientation with respect to time, place, or person.

**Mental retardation.** At the beginning of life is a group of diseases in which physical causes lead to defective function. These are collectively known as mental retardation, which is primarily a deficiency in development of intelligence, though emotional effects may result secondarily. Strictly speaking, it is not a psychosis in the sense of a loss of contact with reality, but it does represent abnormal mental function and therefore needs to be mentioned briefly here. This deficiency is either already present at birth or may occur shortly thereafter. It is not usually recognized, however, until the second year when the child fails to walk or talk. The low intelligence leads to a weak sense of self-preservation, an inability to understand the moral standards and principles of behavior in society, difficulty in learning of any sort, and the consequent inability to get or keep a steady responsible job other than the most menial. In profound cases the children cannot even attend to their own physical needs. This, then, necessitates protective care, supervision, and special training to look after themselves which can be done better in a specially equipped institution than at home.

*Causes of mental deficiency.* There are many causes for mental deficiency, the majority of them occurring before birth. Hereditary or genetic factors are poorly understood and may in fact be less to blame than was formerly thought. The mongoloid child is the commonest in this category and is thought to result from a chromosome abnormality. Defects in the development of the brain in the growing embryo can lead to such conditions as hydrocephalus. German measles in the first three months of pregnancy, toxemia of pregnancy in the last three months, certain glandular disorders, syphilis, and a few other severe infections in the mother can lead to a brain-damaged child. Rhesus factor or Rh blood group incompatibility between husband and wife has also, until recently, caused damage in the second and subsequent babies, but this danger is almost past now thanks to new discoveries and effective prevention and treatment.

A long or difficult obstetric procedure during birth can lead to oxygen deprivation which can result in cerebral palsy or other forms of brain damage. After birth, meningitis, encephalitis, certain metabolic or nutritional deficiencies, or serious head injury can lead to mental retardation. Children with a tested I.Q. of 60 or less should not be raised at home but taken care of by specially trained personnel in an institution where they can be protected from family members lacking patience and understanding.

**Functional Psychoses.** The most serious of the mental diseases are those classified as the functional psychoses. *Functional* means that up to the present time there has not been proven any definite organic or physical cause to explain them. No bacteria or viruses, no biochemical or genetic imbalances or abnormal cell changes have been demonstrated as direct causes. There have been many theories and some evidence, but no proofs. (See subsequent discussion of causes of schizophrenia.) There is much experimental work being done to try to find organic causes. I believe it will be successful. Then it will be easier to treat these conditions.

*Syndrome of functional psychoses.* The word *functional* is used to emphasize that it is the patient's inability to function successfully that is the essence of his disorder. He is apparently out of touch with reality, and he says and does things in a manner which betrays his separation from the real world in which he lives. This leads to inappropriate behavior. What he says and does reveal that he has a disorder of thinking. You can detect this by patiently listening to a psychotic talking for a few minutes without interruption. You will begin to realize that he does not stick to the subject (loss of goal-directed thought), his mind wanders (flight of ideas), he goes off on a tangent away from the first direction of his remarks (tangential), he "beats about the bush" and never comes to the point (circumferential), and it may become so bad that there seems to be no connection whatever between one statement and the next (loosening of associations). His general appearance is liable to be untidy in manner of dress. His behavior, attitude and even facial expression may strike you as being unusual or peculiar. He may have a compulsive ritual, usually some harmless sequence of little actions which he has to do repetitively. He may appear tense or restless, agitated and unable to sit still. He may speak very fast, wring his hands, pace up and down, and even cry. On the other hand he may seem to be very withdrawn, brooding, and unable or unwilling to communicate. In the extreme condition of catatonia he will be totally out of contact with his surroundings, possibly staring blankly into space and unresponsive even to painful stimuli.

If you are with someone whom you fear may be seriously mentally ill, observe carefully his *speech and emotional state,* for these will give you some clues as to when the time has come to help him to get treatment. For example, what he says will reveal a thinking disorder if the production and flow of his thoughts are abnormally fast or slow, if their continuity is not clear, if he keeps repeating the same thing (perseveration), and if he suddenly stops for a few seconds unable to continue (blocking). Also the actual content of what he is saying is often a good clue. Consider these points: Does he persistently talk about himself in relation to everything he mentions (self-referential or autistic thinking)? Does he have any unrealistic convictions that he is being persecuted or is under the influence of outside forces (paranoia)? Does he have any persistent complaints about bodily aches and pains when his medical doctor has thoroughly examined him and said there is no physical illness (hypochondriacal preoccupations and somatic delusions)? Does he hear voices or see things that are not really there (auditory or visual hallucinations)? Does he have suicidal thoughts? This is a very important point. Do not wait until he threatens to make a serious suicide attempt. Even such remarks as, "I'd be better off dead," or "I wish I could go to sleep for a long time," should alert you to the urgency of treatment.

Consider also the patient's emotional state. Is he very depressed, anxious, perplexed, irritable, apathetic, or unusually elated? Does his mood change from "high" to "low" rapidly (mood swings)? Can he control his emotions on social occasions and is his emotional state consistent with what he is saying or doing? Is it appropriate for the occasion? Is there a discrepancy between thinking and feeling (inappropriateness of affect)?

If you live with someone in your home whom you have been able to observe over a period of time, there are some further points, *physical problems*, to consider. What is his appetite like? Has there been any significant weight change lately? Have bowels been regular? Has his sexual interest or performance changed from what was previously normal for him? Does he have difficulty getting to sleep or staying asleep? Has there been a general slowing down in his activities or loss of interest in things he

previously enjoyed? These sorts of changes, if without physical
cause, can often accompany, for example, a psychotic depression.
—In certain forms of psychosis you may notice a *loss of memory*
both for recent and distant events. There may be some disorientation such as in the patient's inability to tell the time or know the
date or where he is or with whom he is speaking. He may not
recognize even people he has known well for years. His intellectual functioning may be impaired and his *judgment and insight
adversely affected.* He may strenuously deny that he is ill and in
need of treatment and it will become necessary for you to point
out to him what changes you have observed to have taken place
before he can be persuaded to go to a psychiatrist's office or a
hospital.

*Schizophrenia.*  By far the most common functional psychosis is
schizophrenia, which is a serious disorganization of the personality structure. It used to be called dementia praecox—*dementia,*
deprived of reason; *praecox,* young—because it was originally
thought to have its origin at puberty and led to a precocious
insanity. The term *schizophrenia* means split mind or split personality. This does not mean, as the common misconception has it,
that the patient feels or acts as if he were two different persons.
The split refers to the separation or difference between the patient's thinking on the one hand and his feelings or affect on the
other. For example, his affect may be inappropriate (such as
laughing while telling of an unhappy occasion), or it may be
stereotyped with rigid unchanging emotions unaffected by differ-
ing situations, or it may be just flat and apathetic. The thinking
disorder of the schizophrenic with its loss of logical processes has
always been regarded as the classical sign of this disease. It may
be autistic, which means subjective, idiosyncratic, self-centered,
and with total disregard for reality, and it may be formed of
dreamlike symbols or be frankly bizarre. In severe cases it may

consist of hallucinations or delusions which are convictions not changeable by reason or logical argument.

Another major subjective problem is the patient's difficulty in separating the real world from his fantasy world. He is not sure where one ends and the other begins. He may not be able to separate his own thoughts or even the concept of his own body from those of others. This is known as a *disturbance of ego-boundaries* and leads to a distortion of his self-identity and an inability to evaluate and deal properly with his environment, known as loss of reality testing. A final difficulty of the schizophrenic is his problem in getting along well with other people. It seems impossible for him to establish lasting friendships. He exhibits a marked ambivalence toward those closest to him. He is not sure if he loves and trusts them or hates and fears rejection by them. This leads to *anhedonia* which is a chronic inability to derive enjoyment from anything he does or get pleasure from the company of friends or loved ones.

The symptoms previously described may be of short or long duration or intermittent. The term *psychosis* strictly means a condition of severe mental disturbance leading to loss of reality contact. Although schizophrenia is classified as a psychosis, in fact, for most of his life, the patient is not actually psychotic. If this were not the case, we would need ten times as many mental hospitals as we have now. Most of a schizophrenic's life is spent in a latent or residual state in which he can function more or less adequately. He may be chronically unemployable but at least he can live outside a hospital most of the time. If he breaks down, "flips out," or undergoes what is called decompensation, he needs to go back to the hospital for a few weeks until he recovers. Thanks to strong antipsychotic medications now available relatively few patients nowadays have to be permanently in a hospital.

Sometimes an apparently normal person might quite unexpectedly and <u>suddenly develop acute symptoms of psychosis as a result of some stressful event in his life</u>. This is known as *reactive schizophrenia*. It is of acute onset, short duration, and usually of good prognosis (good chance of recovery). On the other hand, <u>sometimes the onset of symptoms has been gradual and insidious, starting from early adolescence and not usually precipitated by some external cause</u>. This is known as *process schizophrenia* and is generally of a poorer prognosis. The old traditional classification of schizophrenia into four basic types, simple, hebephrenic, catatonic, and paranoid is still used but other types have had to be added as our understanding of the disease processes has increased. Of these four, the simple and hebephrenic are the process types. The "simple" type, or *schizophrenia simplex*, roughly corresponds with the oldest classical description of dementia praecox. The patient—often an adolescent girl—is apathetic, autistic, withdrawn, ambivalent, indifferent, anhedonic, expressionless in her face, and lacking ambition. She cannot face the responsibilities of adult life, cannot make lasting friendships, becomes chronically unemployed, and eventually ends up unmarried or divorced and needs custodial care in a state mental hospital. She may not have the obvious thinking disorder of most other types of schizophrenics and therefore the realization of her condition by her family is usually late, and energetic treatment is thereby delayed or never obtained early enough to be effective.

By contrast, <u>the other process type, *the hebephrenic*, is perhaps the most serious of all mental diseases</u>. Here the young person has a total disorganization of personality structure, with a severe thinking disorder, flatness of affect with inappropriate unpredictable outbursts of extreme silliness or behavior with giggling, stupid and annoying mannerisms, and sometimes transient delusions or hallucinations. These patients cause extreme disruptions at home and heartbreak in the family before they are forced to be committed to a chronic hospital.

*Catatonic schizophrenia,* one of the reactive types, is usually more sudden in its appearance and is seen in adults rather than adolescents. The patient becomes very belligerent and manifests negative and oppositional behavior. There are really two subtypes recognized, the excited and the withdrawn. The excited catatonic exhibits excessive and sometimes violent muscular activity with furious pacing around and shouting. The withdrawn on the other hand is characterized by long periods of complete physical immobility and inhibition of all voluntary activities even to the point of stupor and mutism when he is so lost in his own little world that he cannot respond to any outside contact. If a firecracker went off near him, he would not even move, let alone show any interest.

The *paranoid schizophrenic* is the man or woman who has delusions of grandeur or persecutions. He has a well-organized delusional system which is absolutely unchangeable to any logical reasoning. He may believe he is some great person and because society does not respond to him accordingly he feels it is ganging up against him. He may become hostile and aggressive as a result of other people's behavior not fitting in with his delusions. Some murderers or other criminals fit into this category, and threats of homicide or other felonious intent should be taken very seriously both by the doctor and the family. Hallucinations and excessive religiosity may be involved. As a general rule, however, he does not manifest the gross personality disorganization of the other types of schizophrenia, perhaps because he projects and ascribes to others unacceptable characteristics in himself. For this reason he may go undetected in society because, with the exception of his particular delusional system, he may be able to present himself as mentally healthy. However, unlike pure paranoia, described later, other schizophrenic symptoms can usually be found if looked for. The prognosis is fair since it is usually of sudden onset in later life, and with good treatment and if the patient had no previous psychiatric problems he will probably get over it eventually. However, there are often relapses needing energetic treatment, but they are usually of short duration.

In addition to these four basic types of schizophrenia it has recently become necessary to expand the classification because of overlapping of symptoms and variations of them with the passage of time. For example, *acute schizophrenic episode* applies to a condition of far more sudden and rapid onset of symptoms than previously described. There is extreme confusion, excitement, emotional turmoil, paranoid fears, and deep depression. The patient needs urgently to be hospitalized, and the condition may either become progressive or a remission may be followed by a recurrence at a later date. Very often, however, he may make a complete recovery within a few weeks and never have any further trouble.

*Latent type schizophrenia* is a diagnosis given to a patient who has some of the symptoms described earlier but who has never actually had a psychotic episode. You could think of him as being potentially schizophrenic but one who has not yet decompensated into the overt state. He has sometimes been loosely described as borderline, incipient, or prepsychotic. In this category is included also pseudoneurotic schizophrenia in which it is believed that there is an underlying psychotic process but it is masked by mainly neurotic symptoms such as severe anxiety, hysteria, obsessive-compulsive behavior, and depression. Chronic undifferentiated schizophrenia is used to describe patients who have a mixture of symptoms with definite psychotic thought processes, affect, and behavior and which do not fit into the other clearly defined categories. *Schizo-affective schizophrenia* is used to describe a patient who in addition to other symptoms has marked manic-depressive type mood swings with periods of alternating excitation or depression. Finally, *residual type* is used to describe someone who has recovered from an acute psychotic episode and although now returned to a relatively normal condition still has the underlying problems which might lead to a recurrence.

Both biological and social forces are probably present in *the causes of schizophrenia*. In the present state of medical knowledge we can say at least this much: There is certainly an inherited tendency toward the disease as evidenced by high concordance of the disorder in identical twins and by diminishing concordance in nonidentical twins, siblings, and half-siblings in that order. Also almost every schizophrenic patient has some family member, living or dead, who has had a history of mental illness. Physiological research is beginning to show a possible correlation between certain biochemical changes in the body and schizophrenia, but a definite causal link between them is yet to be proved. Research into chemical causes of all mental illness is the wave of the future, with marked de-emphasis on psychological causes.

Many schizophrenics come from families in which there is a high degree of marital discord between the parents and in particular there is frequently a history of some problems during the early years in the relationship between the mother figure and the patient. Later discrepancies or inconsistencies between what the parents do and what they say can lead to serious confusion in the mind of the developing child. On the other hand, many normal people without psychiatric symptoms come from bad homes. Also by contrast, in happy normal families where one child turns out to be schizophrenic, his siblings all being without symptoms, it is important for parents to realize the possible biological factors and not reproach themselves with soul-searching self-recrimination.

*Affective disorders.*  The other functional psychoses are the affective disorders, the paranoid states, and psychotic depressive reaction. The affective disorders, in contrast with the schizophrenias which are primarily thought disorders, are characterized by disorders of mood, either of extreme elation or depression. It is these mood states which lead to the loss of contact with the environment that are diagnostic of a psychosis. There does not seem to be a clearly defined precipitating event in most cases.

*Manic-depressive illness.*  Manic-depressive illnesses (formerly called manic-depressive psychoses) usually start in the twenties or early thirties and are characterized by severe mood swings. They are divided into three basic types: manic, depressive, and circular. The *manic type* patient has periods of excessive elation, irritability, talkativeness, flight of ideas and accelerated speech, and mental and physical activity. Between these episodes he may be quite normal or slightly depressed. The *depressed type* has only depressive episodes which are characterized by severely depressed mood and slowing down of mental and physical processes even leading to total withdrawal and stupor. Sometimes they may have anxiety and agitation. They also are usually quite normal between episodes. The commonest manic-depressive illness is the *circular type* which has alternating episodes of both mania and depression. The cycle may vary considerably in intensity, duration, and frequency, not only in different patients but in the same person at different times. The patient is usually well aware of what is going on, but so great is the influence of the mood, be it high or low, that events or reasoning have little effect in bringing him back to normality. It is a form of escape, an emotional divorce from reality. During mania he may feel wildly elated and will say and do whatever he feels like, however inappropriate or socially embarrassing. He may have brilliant ideas, make many telephone calls, squander money he does not have on things he does not need, write grandiose letters to the president, and drive faster than is safe. His energy is limitless and he will wear out his family with worry over what he will do next. By contrast, when he eventually comes down from his "high" and becomes depressed, he will appear markedly sad and withdrawn, all activities will be slowed, he will lose his appetite and ability to sleep well. He may be in so much pain that he will develop ideas of dying and will need hospitalization as a suicidal risk. If the patient does not kill himself in his car when he is high or commit suicide when he is low, his prognosis is nowadays quite good if treated. Modern drug treatment with tranquilizers or antidepressants is becoming very effective in controlling his mood swings. In particular, the recently released *lithium carbonate* is extremely effective in preventing high, hypomanic, euphoric episodes, and moderately successful in smoothing out both the high and low mood swings of the bipolar or circular manic-depressive.

*Involutional melancholia.* Another affective disorder is involutional melancholia, which comes during the "change of life" or involutional period in both men and women. Women are most commonly involved, however, and the characteristics are a very severe depression with agitation, worry, and severe insomnia. There is also abnormal concern about her bodily functions (somatic preoccupation) leading to delusions of impending doom or death. There is great guilt resulting from delusions that she is somehow responsible for all the world's ills and deserves to be punished. She sometimes even pleads to be imprisoned or executed, tortured or starved. To any observer she appears to be seriously ill with profound sadness, anxiety, and fear. She is a very serious suicidal risk and has to be committed to a hospital, against her wishes if she is not agreeable. Prognosis, however, is good if treated. These patients, perhaps more than others, do well after a course of electroshock treatment.

*Paranoia.* The paranoid states (paranoia and involutional para-phenia) are distinguished from other psychoses (such as para-noid schizophrenia) by the fact that the essential abnormality is a delusion which is not associated with other thought disorders except insofar as they occur as a result of the delusion itself. The delusions are usually highly systemized and intricate. An initial misinterpretation of an event may lead to a whole series of com-plex rationalizations, one leading logically into the next, with great internal consistency, until eventually the patient lives in the whole delusional system. The delusions may lead him to believe he is being watched or talked about, that others are out to harm or destroy him or he is being influenced against his will by some outside force. He may believe himself to be another person, usually an important public figure alive or dead, or that unusual changes are taking place in his body totally altering his identity. Outside this delusional system he is apparently completely nor-mal with no other evidence of a thinking disorder. There is fre-quently in a paranoid patient a history of a harsh home back-ground with parents who both loved and beat the child inconsistently, thereby preventing him from learning reward and punishment systems correctly. Prognosis is not usually good, but long-term psychotherapy and the development of a trusting rela-tionship between patient and doctor as a model for other rela-tionships can help considerably.

*Psychotic depression.* Finally, a psychotic depressive reaction is a condition of very low moods following some definite experience such as the loss of a much-loved spouse or one's entire financial resources or the knowledge of incurable illness. It often starts as a normal grief reaction or mourning but continues beyond the usual period and the patient becomes worse, instead of recover-ing as most people would do. It eventually leads to a loss of touch with reality and functional inadequacy, often ending in suicide.

Shock treatment is to date the best therapy though some antidepressant drugs can also be effective. Prognosis is usually good, if treated, for at least partial improvement and some degree of return to normal life.

Shock treatment, confinement in a hospital, heavy doses of major tranquilizers or other drugs, psychotherapy, or simply allowing the patient the passage of time with tender loving care are all the therapy that can be given at present. We do not yet know of anything better. But these are at least better than nothing. Psychiatrists should be humble enough to admit that their profession is in its primitive infancy. Major breakthroughs in the treatment of mental illnesses are desperately needed. Meanwhile we have to do the best we can with what we have got. Some Christians believe that *all* mental illnesses are the results of sin and curable only by divine intervention. I agree with them, but would add that sometimes God either chooses not to intervene or is in some way prevented by the patient himself. Indeed only God can cure schizophrenia, but until he does, I, as a physician am going to do my best with my limited resources to relieve whatever suffering I can with the means at my disposal.

# 5

# SPIRITUAL ILLS: THE ENEMIES OF FAITH

**Spiritual gifts to the believer.** Faith, hope, love, joy, peace —these are some of the great gifts that God gives to the believer in Christ. We do not deserve them nor earn them in any way, but God has obligated himself to give them to us when we yield ourselves in total surrender to his will. Down the centuries devout men and women have experienced these gifts which have added a quality to life lacking before they made individual personal commitments to Christ as Saviour and Lord. This added quality is experienced quite independently of such material concerns as standard of living, personal wealth, good physical health, or social prestige. People from all walks of life, from the highest in the land to the lowliest slave, have been included. Unhappily, however, it is not as simple as it sounds. Even though we receive these gifts they need to be appropriated into ourselves. If I am given a gift of one hundred dollars, it is of no use to me unless I spend it. For as long as it stays in my wallet it is only potentially useful. This is the trouble with so many Christians. The abundant life available in Christ is not being claimed and enjoyed. It is only potential at best. Fleeting glimpses of what it could be like are occasionally seen, but for the most part, life for many Christians is lacking in satisfaction, and they are frustrated by personal problems for which they need help. The next seven chapters deal with some of the particular problems which prevent enjoyment of the abundant life. Professional help may be needed to deal with some of them. Others the Christian must deal with by himself with God's help.

*Damaged faith can lead to damaged emotions.* In chapter 3 the point was made that total health for the Christian includes a right personal relationship wtih God in Christ. For the unbeliever, in whom the spiritual dimension is totally or partially lacking, one must evaluate his mental health on the basis and within the limits of what he has. A complete atheist can be perfectly healthy if health is defined strictly within the limits of physical and psychological well-being. For the Christian, however, if his personal faith is lost or weakened, and his spiritual dimension thereby adversely affected, there may be repercussions in the emotional and psychological areas, and these in turn could lead to physical problems. For this reason anything that damages a Christian's faith should be considered potentially capable of damaging him emotionally and physically as well. Faith, however, is preeminently the cardinal spiritual gift. It is the *sine qua non* of the spiritual dimension. Without it, it is not possible for man to respond to God. He can only search, and without faith all searching is vain. But God searches for man and finds him. Man responds by the faith that God gives him.

*Adverse influence of evil.* It has become obvious at this point that if only God and man were involved everything would be wonderful. This was indeed the situation in the Garden of Eden, but a third personality intervened into the perfect God-man relationship. This personality has been variously described as the devil, Satan, or the rulers of the darkness of this world. It matters not for this argument what you call this being, nor whether or not you believe literally, as I do, in the Genesis story of the existence of a personal devil or hell. The fact of Christian experience is that there is a powerful evil influence trying to prevent us from living the abundant life of faith in Christ. This evil influence is constantly at work trying to undermine our faith either by causing us to doubt the truth of God's Word or by cooling our love and our desire to put Christ first in our lives.

*What faith is and is not.*   Faith is described as a "confident assurance of that for which we hope, a conviction of the reality of things we do not see" (Hebrews 11:1 WEYMOUTH). This is not autosuggestion or some kind of psychological exercise. Nor is it a delusion which causes us to believe something which simply is not true. If it were a psychological delusion, there would be plenty of other evidence that the believer was mentally ill. In fact, however, personal faith is found in the mentally healthy as well as in the mentally ill, further evidence that it is a dimension outside of that which can be adequately described solely in psychological terms. Faith is not contrary to reason. It is above and beyond reason. It is not contrary to logic. It has a logical system within itself. It is not acquired by any human effort. It is a free gift from God requiring only human acceptance for its effect. It can be damaged by the power of Satan, but never totally destroyed. Once the gift has been appropriated by the believer it is his for all eternity. The power of the Holy Spirit is stronger than Satan and God will not allow one of his sheep to be lost. Nevertheless the man of faith needs to guard against certain specific things which can damage his faith and thereby cause spiritual, and thence emotional, problems.

**Selfishness, the basis of sin.**      Selfishness is the basis of all sin. Any particular sin has at its root selfishness, the modern development from the necessary primitive animal instinct of self-preservation. Satan tempted our first parents by suggesting that God's Word was not true, that they would not die as God had warned if they ate of the tree of knowledge of good and evil. Once doubt had been implanted, selfishness took over and caused them to sin. They selfishly craved for something which was not theirs.

The sin of pride led them to think that they knew better than to abide by the commandment of God. The sin of greed led them to steal. It was especially the *sins of pride and greed* that Christ preached against, and it is especially these sins in the Christian's life which can be so destructive to his personal faith. Selfishness leads to pride and greed. Pride leads to self-righteousness, vanity, prejudice, anger, and hatred. Greed leads to stealing, murder, dishonesty, jealousy, gluttony, disobedience, laziness, and immorality. Any of these sins can damage faith and directly or indirectly cause emotional problems in the believer. Almost all of the Christian patients I have seen in my office since I have been in practice have had emotional problems directly attributable to one or more of these specific sins, and without exception they could be traced back to pride or greed and selfishness.

*Spiritual cure needed.* The answer to the problem of selfishness, for the Christian, is found only in his willingess to restore Christ to the lordship of his life. "I am crucified with Christ: nevertheless I live; yet not I, but Christ liveth in me: and the life which I now live in the flesh I live by the faith of the Son of God, who loved me, and gave himself for me" (Galatians 2:20). No psychotherapy or medical treatment can do anything for selfishness. It is not primarily a psychological problem. It is a spiritual problem which needs a spiritual cure. That cure is the power of the Holy Spirit which can restore the new life of Christ in me. With its help I can conquer selfishness and live the victorious and healthy life of faith.

**Demon Possession.** Do I personally believe in demon possession? I am prepared to stick my neck out and say that I definitely do. I have never seen a classic case in Europe or America but I am quite sure that I have in Africa where several years ago I spent some months. I was not able to examine the cases either medically or psychiatrically, nor did I personally observe any dramatic cures by exorcism. However, I believe the testimony of English-and American-trained missionary physicians with whom I have discussed the phenomenon and who have themselves observed, examined, documented, treated, and in some cases permanently cured cases of severe physical, mental, and emotional disruption which could not be fitted into any psychiatric classification. The fact that dramatic instantaneous cures have taken place as a result of the invocation of the Holy Spirit by local Christian leaders on behalf of the patients is itself strong evidence that the original condition was not simply a psychosis as understood by most doctors trained in the twentieth century. One of the reasons for this, I believe, is that demon possession is not primarily a psychological illness. It is primarily a spiritual problem, with physical and psychotic manifestations as incidental by-products. If I am correct that demon possession is a spiritual sickness, then there is no reason why it should not occur in "civilized" countries as well as underdeveloped ones. In fact I believe that it does. Here in America there is plenty of it. The only differences from African experiences are that the psychotic side effects are not so apparent, and we do not usually call it demon possession.

*Inner conflict between good and evil.*  I, in common with over twenty million evangelical Christians in this country and countless millions in other countries, believe strongly, indeed experientially, in the existence and power of the Holy Spirit influencing our thoughts, emotions, and wills. We believe this is an influence for good. Good in the sense that it guides us in the direction of God's will for our lives. Against this influence is a spiritual power pulling in the opposite direction, the power of Satan. "Put on the whole armour of God, that ye may be able to stand against the wiles of the devil. For we wrestle not against flesh and blood, but against principalities, against powers, against the rulers of the darkness of this world, against spiritual wickedness in high places" (Ephesians 6:12).

Yes, there is undoubtedly an evil spiritual power trying to influence Christians in a direction opposite that of the love of Christ in their lives. I and all Christians who desire to surrender our lives totally to Christ have experienced this contrary force. I do not care if you call it original sin, a personal devil, or an evil spirit. It exists constantly as a fact of the Christian life and only the power of Christ can successfully combat it, as recorded in several passages of the New Testament. The inner conflict is the Christian's daily experience.

Demon possession in primitive countries may, incidentally, sometimes manifest itself in a form of derangement similar to a psychosis. Demon possession in America is more subtle, causing Christians to lose their personal faith or effectiveness in witness. The cure comes only from the Great Physician who alone can give the spiritual healing we all need. God's power is greater than that of the devil and its healing force is ours by faith.

**Fasting.** Another area in which spiritual disorders can occur is with the practice of fasting. Jesus fasted and prayed and taught His followers to discipline themselves to do the same. There is no doubt that a brief period of reduced food intake can facilitate clear thinking and mental concentration, such as is needed for prayer. Blood supply diverted from the brain to the stomach unquestionably slows thought processes. Conversely, small meals for a few days during a period of spiritual retreat can help intense devotional exercises. This fasting, however, must be relative and temporary. Total abstinence from all food is physiologically harmful even for short periods, and partial abstinence for a long period can also lead to serious problems in the body's functioning. Not only does prolonged fasting lead to emaciation but it also can cause a significant reduction in the body's defensive abilities to combat infection or injury.

A Christian patient of mine was recently suffering from an emotional disorder called *anorexia nervosa* or nervous loss of appetite. He was desperate to regain the favor of God which he thought he had lost by disobedience. He persuaded himself that by protracted fasting and spending hours in prayer and Bible study he could achieve this. He lost over thirty pounds, became very pale, got depressed, lost his normal cheerful personality, felt physically ill most of the time, and believed all this suffering represented God's continuing disfavor. I pointed out in therapy that God's favor is a gift and cannot be earned by good works. It has to be received and responded to in obedience. I emphasized that he was acting contrary to the Scripture which tells us to take care of our physical bodies because they are temples in which the Holy Spirit dwells. I also had to deal with the guilt and hostility and other problems which had led him to his distressing condition, and I helped him to see that what he thought had been disobedience had actually been the logical results of his neurotic, obsessional, legalistic perfectionism.

Fasting in moderation, occasionally and temporarily, yes. Fasting protracted to the point of serious weight loss and bodily harm, no.

**The Occult.**     Pursuit of the occult is sin; it is essentially idolatry. I make no apologies for being dogmatic. The Old and New Testaments are quite clear on this whole issue. "Thou shalt have no other gods before me" is the first of the Ten Commandments (Exodus 20:3). Superstition, horoscopes, astrology, Ouija boards, mediums, witchcraft, black magic, sorcery, nonmedical hypnosis, clairvoyance, fortune tellers, phrenologists, palmistry,

scientology, and many other forms of "parapsychological" prac-
tices are categorically contrary to the explicit or implicit teachings of Scripture. However, the incredible increase in the pursuit
of these things by sophisticated and well-educated people in this
country basically means one thing: there is an ever increasing
innate conviction by normal people that there is a power outside
of themselves; a power that controls the universe and which can
possibly be of use to help them. Dr. Clyde Narramore of Rosemead, California, has rightly said: "Unwilling to acknowledge his
Creator, the God of Heaven, man is being seduced by Satan into
dependence upon every form and device of superstitious, un-
scientific, idolatrous practice." There is a deeply ingrained need
in man to search for and worship some supernatural power
beyond himself. This fundamental need is seen at all levels from
the most primitive culture to the most developed and advanced
one. It is the responsibility of committed Christians to live the
victorious life in Christ and to witness and boldly testify that this
supernatural power is indeed available to all who would believe
and that it can fully satisfy all one's needs and give the guidance
necessary to deal with all life's situations.

**Ignorance of the future is God's will.**      Ignorance of the future is ordained by God, indeed is a gift from God. I am *glad* I
am ignorant of the future. I live by faith and I trust God that
nothing will happen to me outside of His will and purpose for me
for as long as I desire that that will be done. Can you imagine how
intolerable life would be on this earth if we knew for certain what
things would happen to us in the future? We would be in a
constant state of anxiety or depression. "Where ignorance is
bliss, 'tis folly to be wise"! God has not given us a knowledge of
the future nor the ability to obtain it. In this dispensation we are
limited in knowledge but expected to live by faith. One day we

shall know even as we are known. Craving for knowledge of the future is absolutely contrary to God's will for man and therefore any attempt to obtain it is devil inspired and eventually damaging or even destructive to all who pursue it.

# 6

# DEPRESSION AND DESPAIR: THE ENEMIES OF HOPE

**Depressive Neurosis.** Depression is by far the commonest psychiatric symptom and is found in every stage of mental illness from a temporary depression in a normal person who has suffered a great personal disappointment to the deep suicidal depression of a psychotic. Neurotic or reactive depression lies between these two extremes. It is usually caused by some actual event in a person's life, such as the loss of a loved one, collapse of a business endeavor, or a serious physical illness; but instead of the normal depression, grief, or mourning another would experience, with recovery in a few weeks, the depression stays for several months and can become so severe that the patient is incapacitated to the point that all he wants to do is curl up at home and withdraw from all outside human contact.

*Signs and symptoms.* The early signs of depression are sadness of facial expression, loss of interest in work or leisure-time activities (apathy and anhedonia), restlessness and agitation with easy irritability, and expressions of low self-esteem, worthlessness, failure, hopelessness, shame, self-reproach, and guilt. Physical effects include generalized lethargy, loss of sexual interest, inability to get to sleep or stay asleep, early morning waking, physical fatigue after little effort, multiple complaints of bodily aches or pains, constipation, and poor appetite leading to weight loss. As the depression gets worse, there will be severe slowing of thought processes, withdrawal first from social contacts and then

77

even from close family members, total preoccupation with himself as revealed in his speech, marked diminution of all physical activity, and eventually loss of all communication and responsiveness.

Reactive depression, which is a reaction from a real or imagined loss, is sometimes called *exogenous depression* to distinguish it from *endogenous depression*, which is not apparently precipitated by some event or loss and which seems to arise spontaneously from within, usually in older people, and tends to be recurrent. The signs and symptoms are the same for both, however, and can be distinguished from a psychotic depression by the absence of a thought disorder, delusions, hallucinations, or loss of reality contact.

*Causes of depression.* Dynamically, depression can sometimes be thought of as anger turned against the self or *self-destructive anger.* Often in depression there is underlying rage and resentment unconsciously felt, for example, toward a recently lost loved one. The depressed patient is angered and resentful of the fact that the loved one has deserted him by death. But he cannot express his anger. It is appropriate to express only love for the lost person and grieve that he or she has departed. The ambivalence resulting from both love and rage, with accompanying feelings of guilt, cannot be expressed or even admitted consciously and leads to hostility and anger turned inward. This self-punishment results in depression. Remember that it is also a cry for help, a plea to others to pay the patient more attention or do something for him to alleviate his present situation. The essential problem is that the patient's real self or ego cannot handle the angry feelings adequately. They then either immobilize the ego causing depression or they are rejected into the body causing psychosomatic problems (see chapters 10 and 11). This is why some people alternate between the two continuously. They are constantly either depressed or have some psychogenic physical problem. Well-meaning friends who express sympathy are of little help. They make it even more difficult for the sufferer to express his inner hostility. As the situation gets worse the only alternative to suicide is psychosis. The ego in attempting to retreat from the anger also retreats from reality.

There are many possible associated causes of depressive reactions in addition to internal anger. *Rejection early in childhood* by the mother (for example, in favor of the need to give more attention to a younger sibling) can lead to a pattern of behavior at the age of three or four which is the equivalent of adult depression. The child is told he should love his baby sister and not be jealous of her. He cannot express his resentment, which then results in a self-protective withdrawal. This pattern of behavior throughout adolescence leads to a sulky, resentful personality structure with a tendency toward recurrent episodes of depression. These episodes untreated can last from a few weeks to a couple of years but are usually self-limiting. If they are not serious enough to lead to psychosis or suicide, the patient will eventually get over them. Properly treated they should last only a few days or a week or two.

It is important not to overlook possible *physical causes of depression*. Almost any physical illness, especially if it is of long duration or if the patient is incapacitated, can make him very depressed. It is not only feeling unwell that makes him depressed. It is his inability to function because of his illness that causes a reactive depression. There are two specific physical illnesses which definitely are associated with low mood. Certain cerebral tumors, not large enough to cause neurological signs can cause severe depression. Also, some endocrine gland disturbances can be a cause. The thyroid gland in particular if not working properly can cause a reduced amount of thyroid hormone to circulate in the system. This condition known as hypothyroidism causes a generalized slowing down of all body processes, sluggishness, fatigue, and obesity. The reduction of circulating ovarian hormones during and after the menopause can also cause depression in women. These conditions are the easiest to treat, however, since hormones can now be taken in tablets or by injection to control the deficiency and alleviate the depression. Low blood sugar can also cause depression.

*Treatment of depression.* Treatment of depression depends on the severity. If the patient is so withdrawn that he cannot function adequately, he will need to be hospitalized, especially if he is a suicidal risk. Severely depressed people respond well to electroshock treatment. It is not known how it works, but it seems to clear out anger from the ego and enables it to remobilize itself. Certainly patients begin to feel less depressed after a half-dozen shocks spread over a period of two weeks. Psychotherapy can then maintain the progress once the course is complete, especially if the patient is helped to ventilate his anger, feelings of guilt and low self-worth.

The less severely depressed patient can be effectively treated as an outpatient with antidepressant medications and an intensive short course of directive psychotherapy. This consists of the opposite of sympathizing, tender loving care. The patient needs to be pushed to reintegrate into society. A little bit of gentle bullying, paradoxically, can make him feel better as he responds with increasing activity and contact with others. This must of course be coupled with support and encouragement. Hope has to be mobilized and positive expectations of future success must be the main focus of attention, not the failures of the past.

The family or close friends are valuable aids to treatment. They should not be overly sympathetic but should be, rather, positively encouraging. They should be sympathetic listeners if the patient wants to talk about his problems, but this should be coupled with constant reminders to him to keep contact with others and busy with interesting or enjoyable activities. They should help him in these contacts and activities and try to avoid getting involved in long discussions which center only on the patient. He should be urged to think more about others and to put himself out for the benefit of others as much as possible.

*Suicide.* The family also is as responsible for suicide prevention as is the doctor. They can observe the patient more closely than he can and should watch for the following danger signs: If the patient begins to talk of suicide, this is a significant warning not to be ignored. He may develop an overwhelming sense of guilt and worthlessness. He may become psychotic or confused with disproportionate fears and feelings of unreality and be suspicious and delusional. He may develop bizarre, inappropriate behavior or express absurd physical complaints. Be especially cautious if he starts to drink too much alcohol or if he unexpectedly appears to suddenly improve with increased energy or even a calm euphoria. Suicide almost never occurs at the depth of the depression when the patient is too slowed down or withdrawn to act, but either as he is beginning to go into a deep depression or on the way up out of one when he has some driving motivation and energy available.

Most suicides have a history of some significant family member, usually a parent, who has suicided. It is *not*, however, an inherited tendency. Suicide is commonest at the adolescent or menopausal periods of life. It is the second highest cause of death among college students, next to accidents. More women than men attempt suicide, but more men are successful, partly because their methods are irreversible. Men tend to hang or shoot themselves or jump out of a window. Women tend to use an overdose of sleeping pills or the gas oven, methods which are slower and reversible if caught in time. Eight out of ten suicides have talked about it before the attempt or at least given a recognizable warning to a friend, family member, or doctor. Studies of hundreds of genuine suicide notes indicate that although the victim was very depressed he was not necessarily psychotic. In other words, most suicides *do* know what they are doing. They are not out of touch with reality. They are usually undecided about living or dying, and especially if they choose a slower method, they are gambling with death, leaving it to others to rescue them. For this reason some suicides are actually accidents if, for example, the victim was not found in time as had been calculated. A suicide attempt is either a cry for help or a manipulative gesture intended to influence some individual emotionally close to the patient. It is often intended as an act of revenge in the belief that the one who has supposedly wronged the patient will feel guilt for the rest of his life for what he had caused to happen.

*"The Blues."* At the opposite end of the depression scale from suicide are those temporary minor episodes of low mood sometimes called "the blues" that everyone experiences from time to time. The blues seem to come in regular cycles lasting a few days and recurring every few weeks. The frequency is very variable in different people but in some they are so regular that they are even able to organize their social lives with the knowledge of when the next one is due. The situation in women is, of course, complicated by the menstrual period which can give times of tension or depression in addition to the depressive cycle. The average cycle in men is approximately four to six weeks. The best antidotes to the blue period are, again, activity and human contact. The worst thing to do is to allow yourself to withdraw alone into self-pitying inaction. The best activity is something which is done for the benefit or cheer of someone else. To give pleasure and happiness to someone else, especially if it requires a little effort on your part, is the best possible way to avoid melancholy rumi-

nations. "A merry heart doeth good like a medicine" (Proverbs 17:22).

**Special problems for the Christian.** Even though we Christians usually hate to admit it, depression can affect believers just as severely as nonbelievers. Our denial is caused by our having been taught that the Christian life is one of joy and happiness and that not to have these is surely a sign of unconfessed sin. For this reason, when a Christian gets depressed he has added burdens unknown to the non-Christian. His low mood makes him feel not only cut off from others but also from God. He begins to have doubts about the security of his eternal relationship with God. He wonders if, after all, he really is the true believer he has professed to be. Is he really saved? Are his sins really forgiven? Is he absolutely sure of eternal redemption? Is Christ really his personal Saviour and Lord? His feelings of unworthiness tend to make him fear divine judgment. He will study the Scriptures and do exactly the opposite of what will be helpful to him. He will concentrate his contemplation on those verses which speak of sin and God's wrath and condemnation and will deny the opposite message of forgiveness in Christ. He will repent, confess, and repent again but still feel depressed. The more he spends in prayer in this mood the more he is thinking about himself and his own feelings and problems. He becomes selfish in prayer, complaining to God about his condition and neglecting thanksgiving and intercession for others.

*Personal experience of depression.* About ten years ago I went through a fairly severe episode of depression lasting several months. I used to spend as much as three hours a day on my knees pouring out my soul to God and claiming for myself every verse of promise I could find in the Scriptures. Gradually I began to realize how preoccupied I was with myself and how selfish I was being with my time. Fortunately, during the same period I was often asked to preach or speak at various church-related functions. These forced me to spend time preparing messages applicable to other peoples' problems rather than mine. Eventually of course my prayers were answered, not necessarily in the particular ways I had been requesting, but in ways which in the long run worked out for the best for me. Looking back on that time I can see now that it was a valuable and necessary experience in my personal and spiritual development.

*Christian hope.*  Hope is the antidote to depression: hope in this life that things will be better tomorrow and hope for the future in everlasting life. The Christian believer has this hope. Because Christ was raised from the dead he knows that he also will be raised to be with Him. For today also the Christian's relationship with Christ gives him the forgiveness which removes shame and guilt and restores his sense of self-worth and happiness. "Now the God of hope fill you with all joy and peace in believing, that ye may abound in hope, through the power of the Holy Ghost" (Romans 15:13). The Christian needs to be patient when he gets depressed. He knows that "all things work together for good to them that love God, to them who are the called according to his purpose" (Romans 8:28). He needs only to wait. Waiting is tough. It can be painful. Any test of endurance or chastening is hard and sometimes unpleasant, but eventually relief comes. Confident hope in the coming of that relief helps to sustain him through the trial. "Now no chastening for the present seemeth to be joyous, but grievous: nevertheless afterward it yieldeth the peaceable fruit of righteousness unto them which are exercised thereby" (Hebrews 12:11).

In therapy with a depressed Christian it is vital to establish as early as possible that his mood or feelings have nothing whatever to do with his salvation. Once he has been saved by grace through faith he is forever justified in the heavenly court and need have no fear of condemnation before the throne of God. He must be encouraged to have faith in the fact of his eternal security and not let his feelings cause him to fear its loss. Depressed feelings are strong, however, and in my experience it is not easy to reassure a believer who thinks he has lost his faith. Merely dogmatically telling him that all is well with his soul is not enough. I have found, however, in my practice that depressed Christians respond very well to the *therapy of prayer.* When I believe it will be helpful, I pray with them out loud, usually at the end of a session.

*Specific problems to be dealt with.* Psychotherapy with Christians must not, however, consist only of spiritual answers. There are the practical issues of his problems of daily living which need to be thoroughly discussed and appropriate encouragement, advice, and persuasion given in their necessary proportions. False guilt has to be exposed and dealt with. Sins causing true guilt have to be repented. (See chapter 9.) Resentment and anger have to be admitted and confessed. Past emotional traumas in childhood have to be understood, and his parents, if blameworthy, forgiven by him.

*Hope is from God.* The Christian is able to achieve all the necessary changes to reverse his self-destructive direction. He has the additional resource of spiritual healing power from God to help him in all that he needs to do to get well. Above all he has hope: not merely the hope that things might get better, but the confident, assured hope that God does love him and is working things out for the best in the long run and will never let him down. "For I am persuaded, that neither death, nor life, nor angels, nor principalities, nor powers, nor things present, nor things to come, Nor height, nor depth, nor any other creature, shall be able to separate us from the love of God, which is in Christ Jesus our Lord" (Romans 8:38–39).

# 7
# HOSTILITY AND PREJUDICE: THE ENEMIES OF LOVE

**Love and disorders of conscience.**     In chapter 5 it was emphasized that selfishness leading to pride and greed was the basic cause of sin which separates man from God. Love is the bridge between God and man, and anything which prevents the full expression and flow of love between them will also effect the expression and flow of love between men. Love is the most important quality in a man's life. Anything which hinders a person's ability to give or receive love robs him of that quality. Alienation from God often leads to alienation from others. Love unites people. Hostility and prejudice separate them. These are not only spiritual problems. They also may have serious psychological and emotional effects in the lives of the people involved. They can lead to depression, anxiety, psychosomatic problems, and personality disorders. They are inescapably bound up with the ethical issues of right or wrong. Absolute and relative moral standards are inevitably involved with man's confusion of thinking, difficulty of understanding, and unwillingness to consider the other person's point of view. Hostility and prejudice are disorders of the conscience or superego and lead to the sort of behavior found in what is described as the psychopathic or antisocial personality. This chapter deals with these disorders. The psychopathic personality type is first described and then some of the particular problems adversely affecting loving relationships in Christians will be considered.

**The psychopathic or antisocial personality.** The psychopathic personality does not have a psychosis or neurosis, yet he frequently finds this way to a psychiatrist's office. Quite often he comes not of his own volition but is forced by some authority, either parental or legal, after he has gotten himself into trouble. He is basically hostile and prejudiced against society. His problem is one of social maladjustment which leads to immoral or illegal actions. These actions on his part are performed deliberately and without any apparent feelings of guilt, shame, regret, internal conflict, or sense of responsibility. They are ego-syntonic, that is, pleasurable to him, a fact which militates against reorientating him in a better direction. He is usually a person of above average intelligence who fully understands the implications and consequences of his actions. When caught or confronted with his wrongdoings, he usually admits his transgression but invents incredible excuses to avoid or at least reduce his blame. He knows the difference between right and wrong. Any anxiety or depression that he might feel is the result of having been caught or exposed, or the fear of it, not the result of the action itself. He generally does not care what other people think and his relationships are invariably superficial. He rarely loves deeply and almost never allows himself to become involved in a meaningful love relationship with anyone. He often fails to learn from his mistakes, and ambitions for a successful career or even any definite life goals are very poorly developed. In extreme cases he will lie, cheat, steal, avoid hard work of any sort, be overtly hostile, prejudiced and destructive, and eventually become caught up in a style of life involving alcoholism, drug abuse, sexual promiscuity, and chronic criminal activities.

*Causes of antisocial behavior.* The causes of psychopathic personality development are not clearly understood but some evidence is being produced by medico-legal research work. Constitutional and hereditary factors are hard to prove but it seems as if the majority of psychopaths have a mesomorphic (muscular) body build and they have a higher incidence of abnormal electro-encephalograms (brain wave test) than the normal population. There is also some evidence that an extra "Y" chromosome is present in the genetic structure of many criminals but the significance of this is not clearly understood.

More important is the evidence of experience in their *upbringing*. Statistically, they frequently are found to come from broken homes with missing, divorced, or dead parents. Many of them are illegitimate and suffered from socio-economic or emotional deprivation. Especially well documented is the high incidence of separation from the mother for an extended period in the first four or five years of life. This is the crucial age for the development of a social conscience. If the patient does not have good parental patterns of behavior and teaching with which to identify or imitate at this age, he is liable to suffer from defects in his own conscience later in life. An appropriate balance of love and discipline by the parents is vital. Too little love or deprivation of needs can lead to strivings for immediate gratification whenever opportunities present themselves. Such immediate gratification early in life reinforces this behavior trait later. Too much love or overindulgence can lead to egocentricity and selfish disregard for other's rights.

Parents who themselves tell lies, steal, or live dishonestly are liable to cause the same tendencies in their children, who therefore feel no guilt. The tragedy is that their whole style of life is then perpetuated continuously from one generation to the next. This type of family is called *dyssocial*, as distinct from antisocial. The personality disorder is not so much inherent in the individual as it is a product of the criminal subculture in which he was raised.

Sometimes parents who outwardly live respectable lives unconsciously encourage antisocial behavior in their children. They give *covert approval* to and achieve vicarious gratification from their children's delinquency. Such children do things that the parents cannot do themselves but wish they could. They tell the children how to behave properly and even behave themselves in a socially acceptable manner. Nevertheless, they get across to their children, nonverbally, the message that they do not really expect them to respond correctly. They do this by being ambivalent in their instructions or by an approving facial expression implying the opposite of what is being said or by condoning transgressions without punishment once they have occurred.

**Problems of antisocial behavior and the Christian.** More than in any other area of psychiatry the problem of the disordered conscience is an opportunity for wholesome spiritual intervention. The patients are often wide open to the influence of the teachings of the Christian gospel. Dramatic personality change can take place as a result of conversion to Christ as Lord in their lives. Many years of psychotherapy could not achieve such a change as this can effect.

*Hostility and aggression.* One of the root causes of antisocial behavior is a lack of love. The patient does not feel loved and does not love anyone. He, therefore, cannot feel that he belongs. He is lonely, isolated, and often afraid. This leads to resentment and hostility which are essentially self-protective mechanisms. Hostility, however, is present not only in the psychopath. It is all too evident in the lives of many people who are otherwise psychiatrically normal. Christians are no exception and many of them are living defeated lives because of anger, hate, envy, and a desire for vengeance. Hostility has usually developed over a period of several years and by the time the problem has come to professional attention it is a deeply ingrained part of the personality structure. It grows as a reaction to frustration, injured self-esteem, neglect or rejection by parents or former loved ones, or a sense of having been deprived of love and affection during early years. It can also be caused by deprivation of opportunity, loss of something treasured, or a feeling of missing out on life experiences normally enjoyed by others.

A certain amount of aggression, however, is necessary in one's behavior, but it does not have to be damaging to other people's interests. The *drive to aggression* is as strong as the drive to sex in all normal people. In a cultured society it is essential that this healthy drive be sublimated or directed into appropriate channels. The nonaggressive or passive personality type will be ineffective in his career and personal life. Women, also, are becoming more aggressive, and understandably so. Formerly the man in her life acted on her behalf as the instrument of her healthy aggressive needs. Now there are too many women without a man, and they have to assert themselves directly through the Women's Liberation Movement and by increased involvement in leadership roles in society as a whole.

*Hostility is essentially a misdirection of the normal aggressive drive.* The healthy person is able to direct his aggressive energies into socially acceptable activities, such as sports and hobbies, and to control anger with internal self-discipline. External discipline in the form of law courts and prisons are not final answers to the basic problems of hostility and resentment. They merely temporarily restrain the angry person from harming others in his society, but they do little or nothing to help him to redirect his aggression into a style of living which would be more beneficial both to himself and others.

Hostility in the Christian can be effectively treated, and the energies involved redirected, if he develops a clear understanding of its causes and the resources available to him in his personal faith. The Christian should be *aggressive for God* but not hostile to men. This does not mean that he has to become meek and mild and bottle up his aggressive drive by presenting a false front of sweet, passive charm. So often we tend to picture Christ as a gentle shepherd surrounded by lambs and children. It is better for the aggressive Christian to see Him as the purifier of the temple venting His righteous anger at the thieving money changers or as the Lord of Glory coming a second time at the head of His angelic hosts at the battle of Armaggedon. I prefer the hymn "Onward Christian Soldiers" to the one "Safe in the Arms of Jesus." Both views of Christ are true. The healthy Christian should have them in the appropriate balance for his particular psychological and emotional needs.

If hostility in the Christian has been caused by loss, deprivation, rejection, or damaged self-esteem, he should be helped to remember that as a child of God he belongs to an innumerable company of fellow believers with whom he is going to be spending eternity. Certainly God did not reject him. He died for him and made him a joint heir of the Heavenly Kingdom. "The Spirit itself beareth witness with our spirit, that we are the children of God. And if children, then heirs; heirs of God, and joint-heirs with Christ" (Romans 8:16, 17).

One of the most aggressive of all God's servants was the prophet Jeremiah who vigorously preached against the forsaking of Jehovah by Judah in favor of other gods. To him God said "Yea, I have loved thee with an everlasting love: therefore with lovingkindness have I drawn thee" (Jeremiah 31:3). Jeremiah employed his aggressive energies in the faithful proclamation of the Word of God, and God assured him that He loved him. We in this generation should do no less than to be aggressive for God, secure in the knowledge of His love and protective concern for us.

*Jealousy.*  Special forms of hostility are resentment and jealousy. These are feelings that develop as a result of frustration in achieving a desired object. The trouble is that the feelings cannot be expressed outwardly because it is inappropriate to do so. The obvious *childhood example of jealousy* is the feeling in an older child when a new sibling is born into the family. Attention he formerly had from his parents is diverted to his newborn sister. He is told he should love her, but his true feelings are of hate because she has stolen the attention which was formerly his. Some degree of sibling rivalry is healthy, especially if it stimulates clean competitiveness. If, however, the older child really believes over a period of time that the younger one is his parents' favorite, he will develop symptoms as a defense against his supposed inferior position. He may start acting out serious deeds of disobedience as an attention-getting device. He may say derogatory things about his sister or do things to try to get her into trouble. He may actually try to do physical harm to her. As the children grow up, if the supposed favoritism persists in the patient's thinking, his attention-getting behavior might become delinquent. Whereas wholesome competition is good between siblings, it is very destructive to the loser if the other is consistently praised as the winner. The loser may become very irritable and begin having sleeping difficulties, either insomnia or sleeping excessively as a form of escape. He may either lose his appetite or eat to excess. A significant, unusual weight change in an adolescent should always be medically investigated. The *root causes of jealousy or resentment are feelings of insecurity or inadequacy.* In adult life if these feelings persist they can cripple a person's emotional stability and delay psychological maturity. They can also cause serious psychosomatic problems (see chapter 10).

*Treatment of jealousy* in the child must start with the parents who should be shown how the inequality of their attention and favor is damaging the child emotionally. In adult life the patient needs to be shown the causes of his resentments and to be helped to express them. He has to be helped to understand how a feeling of inferiority leads to jealousy. He should develop a realistic self-concept and appreciate his true worth. These include acceptance of his limitations so that his ambitions and goals will be actually attainable. Striving for something he can never reach is bound to cause disappointment and resentment. To most Christians, jealousy and envy are considered serious sins. I tend to disagree in this respect: the actions that they lead to may indeed be sinful, but the feelings of jealousy and envy by themselves, while they remain within the person's heart and mind, are to be considered, rather, in the category of temptations which cause emotional pain and need treatment, not condemnation. The Christian believer is able, with the help of the Holy Spirit, to accept God's will for his life and to avoid craving those things which are not intended to be his. He should avoid desiring the treasures upon earth, because where his treasure is, there will his heart be also. Convinced that God's will is the best for him, he can victoriously take no thought for the morrow but seek first the Kingdom of God and His righteousness, believing that all things he needs shall be added unto him. (Matthew 6:19, 21, 33, 34 paraphrased.)

*Prejudice.* Prejudice means to prejudge; to come to a conclusion before all the facts are known; to have a fixed opinion based on incomplete information. To go a step further, it also means to stick to one's biased convictions either by denying valid contrary arguments or, worst of all, by deliberately wanting not to know the full truth which could become a threat to preconceived ideas. Included, therefore, in prejudice is not only ignorance but also a lack of humility and a lack of love. The psychopath is hostile to society because he lacks love and has grown up prejudiced against all whom he imagines are allied against him. Prejudice is also very widespread throughout the human race and is one of the basic causes for most conflict between men and nations. Part of it, of course, is *fear.* We are naturally afraid of the unknown and this leads to fear of strangers and foreigners. The more different other people are from us, the more prejudiced and afraid we are. Different language, different skin color, and different cultural traditions and ways of life tend to make us withdraw protectively to our own safe familiar nest.

Evangelical Christians are especially guilty of prejudice against those who are not numbered among them. One of the reasons for this is that we are taught in the New Testament that there is, in fact, going to be a great difference in the next life between those who are redeemed by Christ and those who are not. In this life, too, as expounded in chapter 2 of this book, there is a quality to the communion of true believers which was lacking in our lives prior to our entering into that fellowship. In a special sense we are indeed different from nonbelievers—but that does *not* mean *better. This is the crux of Christian prejudice.* I am not better in any way than my non-Christian friend. I am only luckier that God has given me a personal relationship with him through Christ. Rather than cause pride and prejudice in my heart, this fact should make me humble and grateful and inspire me to spread the good news to others. Because Jesus Christ is my personal Saviour I have a divinely authorized special relationship with all others who share this experience. This, understandably, tends to set us apart to some degree from nonbelievers, but unfortunately it also sets us apart from others who profess to be Christians and who would like to be numbered among us but who are excluded by us because the nature and quality of their religious experience is different from ours. Hence the destructive splits in the church into separate denominations. We use a verse such as 2 Corinthians

6:17 to justify such an exclusive attitude: "Wherefore come out from among them, and be ye separate. . . ." Taken in its context, however, the verse has to do with idol worship and following after false gods. It was never intended to urge mature Christians to separate themselves from the millions who, although less committed, might nevertheless be spiritually hungry inside for precisely that deeper experience into which evangelicals could help them enter.

What are we afraid of? Is our faith so weak that challenges from unbelievers or inquiry from seekers may threaten to harm it? Gospel truth does not need to be defended. It needs to be let loose to conquer the world. Communion and fellowship with other believers is indeed a very precious thing, and much of the happiness of the Christian life would be lost without it. However, in the countries where Christians are in a small minority much of their happiness is found in their evangelistic outreach and efforts to win others to Christ. This, with rare exceptions, is missing in North America and Northern Europe today. We are too comfortable; we are too conservative. The preservation of the status quo is too important to us. To be a Christian, especially if not too zealous a one, is too respectable. Ever since the time of the Emperor Constantine, the right thing to do has been to become a Christian. But now we lack the challenge and zeal of the early church, or the church today in unevangelized areas. It is interesting, however, that it is in those churches where a strong gospel message is preached that membership tends to grow. It is significant that with very few exceptions churches throughout the country with memberships of over a thousand have a reputation for powerful evangelistic preaching. Not to be interested in spreading the good news of redemption in Christ to others is to be prejudiced against them. We have the most wonderful thing to share with the world. We keep it to ourselves because of fear and selfish exclusiveness. If we don't evangelize, we don't care, we don't love, and in the long run our own spiritual lives will become stagnant and our churches will die. *Outreach is life and growth.* Thousands of churches have already died and others are dying today. They are churches where the full gospel is not faithfully preached and where the Scriptures are not diligently studied and expounded. They are churches where the members are too comfortable to accept change, too selfish to propagate the gospel to others, and too prejudiced to welcome strangers of different backgrounds into their midst.

It is not surprising that, as they get older, children from Christian homes tend to rebel and fall away from the faith of their parents. They can see the hypocrisy, the inconsistency, and the prejudice in their parents' lives. Unhappily, they then tend to equate these with the church, and in rejecting their parents' faith they also reject Christ in their own lives.

By contrast those Christian homes in which love is paramount produce sons and daughters who themselves devoutly propagate the faith to their own children. *Christian love* is unselfish and unprejudiced. It is patient and humble, tolerant and understanding. It is giving and giving again. It is the opposite of hostility, resentment, and jealousy. It is the gift above all others which fills lives with happiness, satisfaction, security, and inner peace. It is given by God to all who desire that their time in this world should be spent in a higher dimension. "A new commandment I give unto you, That ye love one another; as I have loved you, that ye also love one another. By this shall all men know that ye are my disciples, if ye have love one to another" (John 13:34, 35).

# 8
# ANXIETY, FEAR, AND STRESS: THE ENEMIES OF JOY

**Differences between neuroses and psychoses.** The neurotic conditions are primarily disorders of the emotions or feelings of which the patient is painfully aware. They are distinguished from the psychoses in which the primary problems are a thinking or psychological disorder, personality disorganization, and loss of reality contact to the degree that the patient is often not aware of his illness. The neurotic thinks and behaves normally and may actually appear to be living successfully as far as his work and even his social and personal life are concerned, but deep inside he is suffering acutely from tension, fear, apprehension, or unhappiness and depression. He struggles to adjust himself to the real world, which he finds a great effort, whereas the psychotic runs away from the real world by drawing into a fantasy world of his own. Even though the neurotic is not mentally ill he has within him bottled-up tensions which eventually express themselves in the form of physical or mental symptoms. These symptoms are therefore like pressure-release valves without which the increasing inner stress could lead to a psychotic breakdown. Untreated neurosis can lead to psychosis, though the frequency of this actually happening is fortunately very rare, and only happens in people already genetically predisposed to it. This chapter deals with the major neurotic symptom complexes of anxiety and its related neurotic types. The conditions are first described and then there are comments on their causes, avoidance, and treatment, and some special thoughts on the Christian's response to the problems when he is affected by them.

*Anxiety Neurosis.* Anxiety is the chief ingredient of all the neuroses. It may be expressed directly or be unconsciously controlled by various psychological defense mechanisms described later. When expressed directly it is called anxiety neurosis. This is an emotional or affective state in which the patient has overwhelming feelings of apprehension, uncertainty, worry, and helplessness which are not caused by any real external danger. During an actual anxiety attack the patient may feel a tightness in the chest, have increased heart and respiration rate, perspire profusely in a cold sweat and very likely tremble, feel nauseated or even vomit or have diarrhea. Such a patient is often treated initially as if he had a heart attack, but an electrocardiogram (EKG) shows that no heart damage has been done. This is not the same as ordinary fear. He cannot explain why he feels like this. It is an all-pervasive feeling of impending disaster, accompanied by intense sensations that he is going to blow up and explode or burst like an overfilled balloon. In extreme cases he becomes completely panic-stricken, loses control, and his behavior becomes totally disorganized.

*Repression of memory.* The cause or causes of anxiety are not well understood. Internal conflict is certainly partly to blame, and this and possible chemical causes will be discussed later. Anxiety reactions are often set off by some situation or event which reminds the patient of some fear he had much earlier in life. Even though the actual precipitating event is relatively benign, it symbolically represents to him a serious threat with which he had previously been confronted such as the loss of a loved object, physical punishment, or even danger of injury or death. In order to protect himself the patient will repress such memories and exclude from his conscious awareness the emotions and impulses which these experiences caused. This repression can lead to a diminution in his ability to think critically, reason logically, or make mature decisions. The condition may not be limited to such acute attacks, however, but be a constant low-grade state of dread which can exhaust the patient and make him feel chronically fatigued so that he cannot concentrate on his work, eat properly, or sleep well. It is exceedingly uncomfortable, even intolerable, because of the helplessness associated with it. For this reason defense mechanisms are put into action to try to mitigate its effects. It is these defenses which lead to some of the other neuroses.

*Hysterical Neurosis.* In this condition there is a loss or disorder of some physical function as a symbolic resolution of emotional conflicts. An example is a teen-age girl I saw recently who wanted to hit her father when he refused to let her go out on a date. She was enraged, but also felt very guilty and frightened of her impulse to strike back. A few mornings later she awoke to find her right arm paralyzed. She had converted her conflict to a physical symptom which represented admission of guilt and self-punishment. This was easier to live with than the conflict and represented a primary gain. An obvious secondary gain was the increase in attention and sympathy she got from her parents. The basic unhappiness remained, however, until psychotherapy penetrated the mask which the symptom represented. In this example a muscular function was affected. Another common one is loss of speech. Altered sensation can also be a conversion symptom, either anaesthesia (loss of feeling), hyperaesthesia (heightened feeling), or paraethesia (abnormal prickling sensations). Blindness, deafness, tics, tremors, and even seizures can also occur. Whatever the conversion symptom may be, it is usually of sudden dramatic onset and the patient often shows a characteristic lack of concern (*belle indifférence*) about it. It is important to distinguish conversion hysteria from psychophysiologic disorders to be described later which are due to actual changes in the nervous system, and from malingering which is done consciously and deliberately.

***Phobic Neurosis.***  A phobia is somewhat similar to anxiety except that it is focused onto a particular object, place, or event. For example: claustrophobia is fear of enclosed places, acrophobia fear of heights, pyrophobia fear of fire, and nyctophobia fear of night or darkness. The patient knows consciously that he is not in any real danger but his symptoms in the situation are very akin to those described in an acute anxiety attack. Although it is quite normal for people to be afraid of certain things such as snakes, driving dangerously fast, walking alone at night, et cetera, the phobic patient will realize that the intensity of his fear is irrational, but he cannot do anything about it. His terror may be so great that he will go to great lengths of inconvenience or discomfort to avoid his phobic object. It can even get to the point where he is unable to leave his house. He will then be as terrified of stepping outside his front door as a normal person would be of stepping out of a speeding car or express train.

There are many things that the phobic person can focus upon. Almost anything that a person can be afraid of can become an object of morbid fear for the phobic patient. Some well-known ones are subways, elevators, high places, crowds, flying in airplanes, et cetera. His fear has been displaced to the phobic object or situation from some other one of which he is not consciously aware. This *displacement* enables him to escape intolerable diffuse anxiety by concentrating it on this one object that he can then avoid. The specificity of the fear, confined to one situation, makes it tolerable and the rest of his daily activities can continue unaffected. A secondary gain of phobia, as with hysterical conversion, is increased sympathy and attention from others. Tranquilizers and occasionally hypnosis have been used to reduce the symptoms, but curative treatment will usually necessitate long-term psychotherapy which must be directed toward discovering both the origin of the underlying anxiety and the reason for the patient having picked his particular phobic object. His secondary gain should also be brought to his awareness because not only his own life but that of others close to him may have been significantly affected by his illness.

*Case report of elevator phobia.* I had a patient a few years ago who had not been in an elevator in fifteen years. We engaged in an intensive course of treatment which consisted of a gradual explanation of the cause of his phobia and actual increasing exposure to it. I first made him intensely imagine himself inside an elevator and then went into one with him. Later we rode several elevators together and eventually he was able to go by himself. The last I heard from him, he had just been to the top of the Empire State Building, and he had *not* climbed the stairs! Treatment was successful because he had been desensitized gradually to his fear until he realized both emotionally and intellectually that it was unrealistic.

*Obsessive-Compulsive Neurosis.* An *obsession* is a recurring thought or idea which keeps on intruding into conscious awareness, is outside voluntary control, and can become very disturbing to a patient's daily routine. Even more disruptive is a *compulsion,* which is a recurrent action or ritual which is repeated constantly as a means of avoiding anxiety. Obsessions and compulsions usually coexist and may be mutually dependent, the one leading to or resulting from the other. An example is the person who has the obsession that disease germs keep floating onto his hands from the air, and this leads to a compulsion to wash his hands frequently. The situation may become so bad that if he cannot quickly find a bathroom with water, soap, and towel, he will become very agitated and develop the symptoms of an anxiety attack. His anxiety will at once subside, however, as soon as he can wash his hands, but the problem may occur again so frequently during the day that his work and all activities become severely disrupted. The patient usually realizes that his obsessions and compulsions are nonsensical but he is powerless to avoid them, indeed he feels better if he gives in to them. The degree of severity of this condition can vary from little more than that of an obsessional personality type to a frank psychosis. It is a defense against anxiety which usually accompanies some hostile feelings connected with authority figures—a struggle with parents or the control of impulses. As with phobic reactions, the treatment usually requires long-term psychotherapy.

*Neurasthenic Neurosis.*    Neurasthenia is a condition in which there is a mixture of neurotic symptoms. Feelings of pressure in the back of the head and down the neck and back are often complained of. The patient usually feels chronically weak and is easily fatigued and even exhausted, without there having been any significant physical or mental exertion to account for it. It is genuinely distressing to the patient, unlike hysterical neurosis, and although there is depression this is not the prominent symptom. Because of its low-grade intensity it may take years for the patient to realize he needs psychiatric treatment. Meanwhile he goes from one doctor to the next and is told repeatedly that there is nothing wrong with him. He is usually basically unhappy and maladjusted and may be a borderline schizophrenic without psychosis. He often becomes a chronic invalid and a burden on his family who are forced to cater to him, wait on him, and worry over him. He is usually unemployed or can keep a job for only a short time.

*Hypochondriacal Neurosis.*    The hypochondriac is similar to the patient with neurasthenia except that his preoccupation with his body and its imagined ills is a predominant and more severe symptom. The wide variety of presumed diseases and bodily malfunctions he persistently complains of can even lead to major abdominal surgery or similar drastic therapeutic interventions, all with only temporary relief. Sometimes strong directive therapy from a doctor he trusts can eventually stimulate and inspire him to conquer his avoidance mechanism and return to responsible functioning.

***Depersonalization Neurosis.*** The depersonalization syndrome, or group of symptoms, consists of feelings of unreality and of separation of part of the self from the body and its surroundings. It is commoner in women and at puberty. It is as if the patient sees herself standing apart and viewing herself and her environment with detached interest. It is a form of withdrawal from reality, usually from some unpleasant life situation and is most often found in an insecure but probably otherwise normal individual. Prognosis is good since it is usually of short duration. Treatment consists essentially of helping her to gain understanding of the origins of her disorder and stressing her obligation to live realistically.

***Causes of anxiety.*** There are probably more theories about the causes of anxiety than about any other diagnosis in the whole of medicine. Several schools of thought have tried to dominate psychiatry over the last fifty years and most of their differences are in the area of the origin and treatment of the neuroses. No one has all the answers, but each theory is at least a partial explanation of the problem as a whole. For example, the classical psychoanalytic explanation of anxiety by *Freud* and his followers is that it is the product of internal conflicts between the id and the superego which the mediating ego is unable to reconcile. The conscience and the basic drives of aggression and sex, when pulling in opposite directions, lead to anxiety when no compromise is reached. Anxiety therefore is a reaction of the ego which serves the purpose of warning the individual to take appropriate action to deal with the stressful situation. *Karen Horney* taught that anxiety is the result of personal and collective insecurity. *Harry S. Sullivan* emphasized that it was caused by disturbances in our interpersonal relationships, especially if they involve rejection or disapproval by others which lead to loneliness and loss of self-esteem. *Eric Fromm* considers anxiety the result of meaninglessness in many people's lives. In his existentialist thinking *Rollo May* says that anxiety is apprehension of the future (culminating in death) with the confrontation of decisions that have to be made as a result of planning for it. Anxiety can also be a result, of course, of a real or imagined danger whether the threat is to physical safety or to one's security in other areas.

All anxiety or psychic tension is not bad however. A little of it in normal amounts can enhance performance. Athletes would be unable to perform successfully without it. Businessmen do better in their competitive world than they could do without its stimulus. It definitely strengthens concentration and spurs imagination, thereby producing more creative ideas. It stimulates interest and develops ambition. It protects from danger. Too much, however, can actually decrease performance. It can dampen reasoning abilities, dull imaginative thinking, cause discouragement, and take the joy and peace out of a person's life. It can also cause psychosomatic symptoms like an upset stomach, palpitations of the heart, headaches, cramped muscles, and a variety of vague aches and pains all over the body.

Investigations into *hereditary or genetic factors* in the etiology (causes) of anxiety are not conclusive enough to make a clear case that anxiety-prone people tend to run in families. There is the obvious fact, of course, that anxious parents raise anxious children, but this would probably be due more to environmental influence during their upbringing than any congenital tendency.

The most important area of investigation at the present time is the connection between *chemical factors* and anxiety attacks. Much work has yet to be done but this much is known: There is a definite connection between feelings of fear, tension, apprehension, or anxiety and the concentration of norepinephrine (a form of adrenaline) in the circulating blood. This norepinephrine together with other chemicals such as serotonin and dopamine are involved in the transmission of impulses among nerve cells within the brain and between the brain and the rest of the body. Emotional responses and resultant behavior are initiated in the area of the brain called the hypothalamus. This is fed information from the higher centers such as the cerebral cortex where incoming sensory data are sorted out. For example, if I hear or see something dangerous, the information goes via the auditory or optic nerves to the cortex. There the facts are instantaneously evaluated and relayed via intermediary centers to the hypothalamus. It then sends impulses down cranial or spinal nerves to the muscles or down the autonomic nerves to affect changes within the body. The individual then reacts appropriately by dealing with the dangerous situation either by direct response or avoidance. If it is not so dangerous after all, he will be programmed to relax instead. Norepinephrine and the other chemicals are involved in the synapses (junctions) of the various nerve cells involved in the reflex action described. If, however, there is too much norepinephrine when there is no danger, there will be an overreaction or unnecessarily exaggerated response. This is an anxiety attack. It is a state of fear. Once it starts, it stimulates more norepinephrine production. It is then a vicious circle. The sufferer is afraid of fear itself. The physical symptoms then become far worse than the initial stress that started the cycle going.

*Stress.*   At this point something should be said about stress. Although some people experience anxiety without stress, the vast bulk of human suffering in the form of nervous tension or apprehension is caused by the various emotional stresses and strains of daily living. Generally speaking, stress is worse in this generation than in most previous ones. The pace of life in the twentieth century is certainly much more stressful for most people than it was one hundred years ago. Urban living is generally more stressful than suburban or country living. The hostility, rudeness, and selfish behavior in crowds is inevitable in cities. Noise is very stressful. Fire and police sirens, construction and repair squads with compressed-air drills, trucks and motorcycles, buses and subways—all add to the constant stress of city life. The poor have anxiety about how to make ends meet, but the rich are anxious about their investments, business deals, and the state of the market. Unemployment and physical illness are great threats to one's tranquility. Hatred, boredom, frustration, and fatigue are common causes of internal stress. Stress is the wear and tear of life, but it is not the stress itself but the effects it produces on our bodies and minds that are damaging. Some stresses are good. A game of tennis, a thrilling movie, or an exciting happy piece of news are stresses which, like anxiety, cause rapid heartbeat, but they are not damaging in reasonable quantities. Some stress is necessary. We are at our least stressful on first waking in the morning. We have poor physical coordination and some mental confusion initially, but the stress of having to get up and dressed for the day helps us to pull ourselves together quickly.

*Avoiding stress.*   To what extent are stress and anxiety avoidable? Obviously patients suffering from full-blown anxiety neurosis with uncontrollable episodes causing acute attacks need professional treatment. But most anxiety in response to stress in any form can be avoided or dealt with without a doctor or psychiatrist. Here are some commonsense suggestions which are fairly obvious but often overlooked.

1. Face up to and *accept reality.* Take a hard honest look at the things you fear. Acknowledge the fact of the stress they cause and don't let your reaction to it be worse than the fact itself. Change what you can and don't be frustrated by what you cannot change. Accept it and adapt yourself to it. Ninety percent of what you are afraid of will never happen.

2. *Divert attention from yourself.* Distract yourself from morbid, pessimistic, self-destructive thoughts. Quit self-pity. Read something that interests you or do something enjoyable. By any means think about something other than yourself and your sufferings. Learn to laugh at yourself with your petty problems.

3. When stressed with boredom, monotony, or fatigue do the dull or difficult tasks first. Leave yourself the more easy or pleasant ones to the end. Loaf a little. *Take occasional breaks* doing something relaxing or enjoyable. Do *not* overeat or drink. They are very poor methods of escape.

4. Work can be addictive. Hard work is good and healthy but some *diverting recreation* is essential for a balanced emotional life. Develop hobbies or interests you can look forward to when the day's work is done. Budget time. Time for work, time for play, time for sleep. Eight hours of each every day is ideal.

5. *Get enough sleep every night.* A minimum of seven hours for an adult is necessary. Eight is preferable for adults, essential for adolescents. Don't go to bed in a state of emotional turmoil, worry, or tension. Forget the day's problems and make up after the argument with your spouse before turn-

ing in. Take sleeping pills only as an absolute last resort and
then only if prescribed and supervised by your doctor.
Strictly avoid all self-medication.

6. *Talk through your problems.* Get them off your chest. Share
   your problems with your wife or husband. Ask advice of a
   trusted friend or family member. Tell your priest or minister about your difficulties even if you think he cannot help.
   Don't be too proud to have a few sessions with a psychiatrist
   or professional counselor.

7. Make sure your *vacations* are times of complete change from
   your daily routine. They can be quite energetic and far from
   relaxing. The important thing is that they should be different. If your doctor recommends it, don't be resistant to
   taking a few days medical leave of absence. Impending nervous breakdown from emotional stress is just as much a
   medical condition as a broken leg or the flu. Get right away
   for a short break and do new things.

8. Have regular medical checkups, and if your doctor author-
   izes it, take plenty of *exercise.* Keep fit. Keep your weight
   down. Keep your heart and lungs in good shape and your
   muscles toned up. (See chapter 10.)

9. Don't neglect the spiritual side of your nature. *Regular church
   attendance,* even for those who are really not sure just what
   they believe, can be a refreshing source of inspiration, challenge, encouragement, and comfort.

**Treating anxiety.** Treatment of anxiety by the doctor should not
be underestimated. Patients who do not get well quickly sometimes become very impatient at their apparent lack of progress.
This is especially the case if they are paying a lot of money for
their treatment and they do not see that the doctor is helping
them much. The fact is, however, that the patient's feelings of
helplessness, apprehension, imminent danger, loneliness, and

frustration would be far worse if he did not during the crisis period have the security of knowing that at regular intervals he could unburden his thoughts and feelings to someone who he believed really cared and was equipped by training and experience to help him. The doctor on his part must convey understanding, sympathy, confidence, ability to help, and genuine concern. Once the patient is sufficiently confident in his doctor's ability and care he can pour out his fears and admit to other emotions that are troubling him such as depression, hostility, anger, and guilt. As the patient does this, the doctor uses a skillful blend of authoritative persuasion, suggestion, and directive advice with supportive reassurance and nondirective sympathetic listening and understanding. Psychotherapy of anxiety sometimes can produce quick results if the patient's ego strength can be built up rapidly to a level of effective functioning. Others need constant support and encouragement over a period of several months or years. Short-term intensive therapy usually necessitates visits to the doctor twice a week at least. Long-term therapy can be handled on a less intensive, once or twice a month basis.

*Drug therapy* is a boon. It is fortunate that powerful tranquilizers are now available for doctors to give patients suffering from anxiety. It would be impossible for all to be seen by psychiatrists. It is estimated that about 5 percent of the population at one time or another experience some symptoms of anxiety. This works out to forty patients to every practicing physician in the country. Without drugs to prescribe, the situation in doctors' offices would be chaos.

Drugs work essentially by preventing the damaging side effects of too much norepinephrine and other substances such as lactic acid in the blood. At the synapses where norepinephrine acts as an excitatory transmitter of nervous impulse certain drugs are thought to act as antagonists to prevent or at least reduce this effect. Conditions in which anxiety is complicated with concurrent depression do well with drugs which have both antidepressant and tranquilizing actions.

**The Christian and fear.**     *Anxiety is not a command of God.*
The Christian faith is not only concerned with reconciling God and man. It is also a practical force which can help man to travel through his earthly pilgrimage. John Bunyan's *Pilgrim's Progress* although written over three hundred years ago is still the greatest classic description of the loving support and help that God gives the Christian on his life's journey. Despair and fear are confronted and dealt with. The same can be true for believers today. We are constantly reassured in the Bible of God's uninterrupted, providential, protective love and care for His children. Indeed, we are actually commanded to "fear not" more than three hundred and fifty times in the Bible. This can be achieved if, instead of fearing men or circumstances, we were to fear God. Fearing God means to have reverential trust and faith in Him and to believe that He is on our side. The more I fear God, the less I fear men. A memorial to Lord Lawrence in Westminster Abbey states of him, "He feared man so little, because he feared God so much." David sang: "What time I am afraid, I will trust in thee. In God I will praise his word, in God I have put my trust; I will not fear what flesh can do unto me" (Psalms 56:3,4). A few hundred years later the prophet Isaiah, giving encouragement to Israel from God, wrote: "Fear thou not, for I am with thee: be not dismayed; for I am thy God: I will strengthen thee; yea, I will help thee; yea, I will uphold thee with the right hand of my righteousness" (Isaiah 41:10).

*Power of prayer.*  It is no good saying to someone having an anxiety attack, "Relax; don't worry. Everything is going to be all right." If he could relax and stop worrying, he would do so. Likewise the anxious Christian needs something more than merely a head knowledge of a few key verses of Scripture, helpful though these may be. The Christian has in fact access to that something more. He can go to the doctors and have psychotherapy and he can take tranquilizers like anyone else, but the something more for him is the therapeutic effect of direct access in prayer to the throne of God. He can unburden himself to God, who not only listens with no time limitation and for no fee but is able to give him peace of mind and the ability to accept his trials and tribulations. God never promises to take our sufferings from us. He does promise to give us the strength to live with them. Anxiety is overreaction to problems. God helps us to face up to them and to accept or change them where possible without anxiety.

Three times Paul asked God to remove his "thorn in the flesh" but He answered him: "My grace is sufficient for thee: for my strength is made perfect in weakness. Most gladly therefore will I [Paul] rather glory in my infirmities, that the power of Christ may rest upon me" (2 Corinthians 12:9). For the rest of his life Paul suffered from his thorn but he did not let lack of faith destroy him with depression or anxiety about it. He said to the Philippians: ". . . I have learned, in whatsoever state I am, therewith to be content. . . . I can do all things through Christ which strengtheneth me" (Philippians 4:11,13). His total trust in God enabled him to be, as can be all believers, ". . . more than conquerers through him that loved us" (Romans 8:37).

Some of the most beautiful words of assurance come to us from Jesus himself. In the Sermon on the Mount He said: "Consider the lilies of the field, how they grow; they toil not, neither do they spin; And yet I say unto you, That even Solomon in all his glory was not arrayed like one of these. Wherefore, if God so clothe the grass of the field, which to day is, and to morrow is cast into the oven, shall he not much more clothe you, O ye of little faith?" (Matthew 6:28–30).

*Love leads through peace to joy.* Anxiety, fear, and stress are indeed the enemies of joy in our lives. Christ intended us to have joy in our relationships with Him. On the way to the Garden of Gethsemane He said to His closest followers: "If ye keep my commandments, ye shall abide in my love; even as I have kept my Father's commandments, and abide in his love. These things have I spoken unto you, that my joy might remain in you, and that your joy might be full" (John 15:10,11).

# 9
# GUILT, TRUE AND FALSE: THE ENEMIES OF PEACE

**Components of guilt.**     Guilt is an uncomfortable feeling. It is a mixture of many emotions and thoughts which destroy inner peace. It is partly the unpleasant knowledge that something wrong has been done. It is partly fear of punishment. It is shame, regret, or remorse. It is resentment and hostility toward the authority figure against whom the wrong has been done. It is a feeling of low self-worth or inferiority. It leads to alienation, not only from others but also from oneself because of the discrepancy between what one really is and what one would like to be. This leads to loneliness and isolation. Guilt, therefore, is partly depression and partly anxiety. It is partly true and partly false. All of these factors, and sometimes several others in individual cases, are seen wrapped up together in the thoughts, both conscious and unconscious, and in the feelings of a person suffering from guilt. In the case of true guilt, for the Christian, the whole situation is made worse by a temporary separation from communion with God. In the case of false guilt there is the erroneous belief that there exists that separation even though that is not actually the situation.

*Guilt, self-hatred, and false beliefs.*  Guilt is, unhappily, very common. It is no exaggeration to say that well over half of my Christian patients have guilt as part of their symptom complex. Very often it is the main trouble as is discovered as we talk through the various problems initially complained about. Self-hatred is an

113

element here and this leads to great difficulty in accepting forgiveness. This in turn leads, of course, to other erroneous beliefs. The Christian's concept of absolute and relative moral standards is twisted and his beliefs about God's revelation to him as an individual may become distorted. Assurance of salvation is often lost.

Many patients who make no profession whatever of Christian belief also have guilt feelings as one of the underlying causes of the depression, anxiety, or low self-esteem that they come to see me about. Just as fear of the future leads to anxiety, worry about the past with fear of retribution leads to self-punishing guilt feelings.

*Relationships of guilt to physical symptoms.* Physical illness is often considered a form of punishment, a product of guilt feelings about some wrongdoing in the past. Some failure, dishonesty, laziness, thoughtlessness, lack of love, or selfish act—chronically infecting the mind and emotions from years back—leads to guilt feelings which cripple and even destroy a person's peace within. All these can not only cause physical illness but prevent its cure when it is seen as punishment. If the physical pain is in fact removed by medical treatment, another one will develop shortly afterward. Psychologically and emotionally it is easier to tolerate the physical pain than the burden of guilt which has thereby been repressed. The pain may be not so much a physical hurt or ache as an erroneous self-concept. Guilt can cause someone to feel ugly when he is not, inadequate in any area of functioning when he in fact has great abilities, weak when he has great strength, or in any way inferior or unacceptable to others when in fact his friends and colleagues think highly of him. Not until psychotherapy can help the patient recognize this self-destructive defense mechanism will he be relieved of both the burden and the pain.

*The conscience and the superego.* In terms of the psychological mechanism involved, guilt stems from the conscience or the superego. Conscience is the innate knowledge of right and wrong possessed in varying degrees by all men. Even the most heartless psychopathic perverse criminal has some conscience which can guide him if he allows it in certain circumstances. The sugerego, first described by Freud, is that component of the personality which develops in childhood as a controlling influence on behavior. It is molded by the restraints and condemnations of authority figures, preeminently the parents, who dominate the early life of the child. Its purpose is to prevent the ego, the real self, from responding unreservedly to the demands of the id, the basic nature with all its sexual and selfish aggressive drives, so that damage is not done either to the person himself or to the society in which he lives. In theory the ego balances the demands of the id with those of the superego so that a compromise is reached. The compromise is not usually totally acceptable to either side, hence internal conflict which leads to many of the emotional problems already described.

The great desire today, especially among young people, to be free and liberated from the restrictions of superego control tends to lead to actions which are later regretted. There has to be a balance. The opposite extreme is that of the person brought up in a very tight, morally restrictive home who thereby develops a superego so strong and unyielding that it becomes impossible for him to give healthy expression to his natural cravings. Examples are the Orthodox Jews with their rigid style of life, overly dogmatic Roman Catholics with their excessive scrupulosity, imposed they believe, by traditional church standards, and ultrafundamentalists and certain heretical Protestant-like sects. Their literal unwavering adherence to the finest points of first century Biblical admonitions leads to intolerable conflict when attempts at perfection in personal conduct fall short of what is realistically attainable in an imperfect world.

***Perfectionism, legalistic Christians, and forgiveness.*** Perfection in this life is categorically impossible. If it were possible, we would need no redemption in Christ. But striving toward perfection in the sense of trying to live a life in conformity with the will of God is not only possible but our aim as Christians. Complete perfection, meaning no separation from a Holy God, is the gift of glorification which we receive only after that great legal arraignment before God's throne in which we are pronounced guilty but are justified by the shed blood of the Lamb of God. We cannot attain perfection but we must strive toward it, not in the sense of trying to earn our salvation by good works, but as an act of gratitude to Christ for having already saved us by His atoning death. Unhappily, legalistic Christians cannot see this. They know it in theory. They have heard it a hundred times from the pulpit, but they have great difficulty accepting forgiveness. They are often people whose parents were very demanding, never satisfied with their efforts, and unforgiving of their failures. These emotional pressures, especially on impressionable, sensitive, and vulnerable children, lead to an inability in adult life to believe that it is possible to be forgiven. They think that forgiveness is something for nothing. This is erroneous. Indeed it costs nothing to become a Christian initially, but it costs everything to *be* a Christian and live up to the pledge made at the moment of commitment to Christ. It costs absolute surrender of the will to God to live the sort of life, albeit imperfect, which God intended for us in this present world. Paul specifically admonished the Galatians against legalism and perfectionism in his letter to them. They were teaching the heresy that good works were necessary to supplement the redemptive work of Christ in salvation. Paul wrote: "Received ye the Spirit by the works of the law, or by the hearing of faith? Are ye so foolish? having begun in the Spirit, are ye now made perfect by the flesh?" (Galatians 3:2–3). To the Romans he wrote: ". . . by the deeds of the law there shall no flesh be justified in his sight" (Romans 3:20) and to the Colossians: ". . . ye are complete in him, which is the head of all principality and power" (Colossians 2:10).

*Repentance requires humility.* Peace and freedom in Christ are had by admitting and repenting quickly for all failures, however frequently they occur, and pressing on to the next step in the confidence that there is not only full forgiveness for the past but also unlimited power available for the future. This may sound too simple an answer. Surely one cannot get rid of guilt that easily. This is true: it is not in fact either simple or easy. Repentance requires both humility and a willingness to avoid repetition. Humility does not come easily to anyone, and Christians are no exceptions. It sometimes takes years of spiritual development for a Christian to reach the point where he can be humble enough before God to admit to his total depravity and to acknowledge that all the good in him is not to his own credit but is only the result of his willing responsiveness to the power of God flowing through him. When the Christian cannot merely profess this, but from the depths of his soul unreservedly believe it, he is a long way toward being able to accept the total cleansing from God which alone can forever remove the burden of guilt from his mind and the depression and anxiety which so often accompanies it.

**True guilt.** We need now to have a clear understanding of the differences between true and false guilt. Generally speaking, conventional psychiatry and psychoanalysis do not admit to the existence of true guilt. Psychiatrists prefer to talk about guilt feelings, not guilt itself. To admit that guilt itself exists would be to admit that there is in fact an absolute moral standard against which we compare ourselves unfavorably. To avoid this admission makes psychotherapy easier, because all behavior can then be evaluated in terms of relative, not absolute, values. It is not necessary, then, to help the patient find answers to the problem of real guilt but merely to help him understand the reasons he feels the way he does. The theory is that once he understands why he feels guilty he will be able to accept the facts as part of his unchangeable past and not let them bother him anymore. Conscious and unconscious conflicts are brought to the surface of full awareness in the expectation that such insight will enable the patient to live at peace with them. Unfortunately this theory very often does not work in practice. Any psychological theory which denies the Biblical concept that there is in fact a divine standard for man's behavior is limited in its therapeutic effectiveness precisely because it is virtually impossible to forget about serious past guilt-provoking transgressions. The memory is a stubborn part of the mind. To try and forget past wrongdoing cannot be done. Only forgiveness can give peace. Forgiveness from the man who has been wronged can help greatly; forgiveness from God can eradicate guilt feelings completely. It is amazing how frequently Christians can testify that guilty memory actually disappears after full confession and restitution have been made and forgiveness obtained. Traditional psychoanalytic theory does not concern itself with the issues of right and wrong. Moral principles are regarded as merely relative and convenient for our culture and not relevant in the consideration of how a man should behave. Psychoanalyists are especially defensive if one should suggest that moral standards are not relative but absolute and that those absolute standards are derived from divine revelation. They say that it is not what is right, but what is healthy, that is the prime consideration. It does not take much imagination to see what chaos our society would quickly evolve into if everyone did what he considered to be healthy instead of what is right.

*Definition of true or real guilt.*  True guilt is the subjective experience of someone who has actually broken the law, the law of man or the law of God. There is nothing false or "pseudo" about it. It is a real emotional aftermath and also a conscious awareness or knowledge of the fact; the fact that something has been done which transgressed the laws of man and society and the law of God. Breaking the law of man is called a crime. Breaking the law of God is called a sin. Breaking man's law can only be satisfactorily dealt with by due process of law, leading to conviction and punishment or to acquittal, the human, legal equivalent of forgiveness or judgment of innocence. The criminal who escapes detection and never comes to trial is in danger of having the guilt of his crime forever hanging over him. Even if the guilt itself is not too great a burden for him, he has to live with the constant fear that he might one day be found out and end up either as a prisoner or as a fugitive from justice.

Breaking God's law can only be dealt with by eternal separation from Him or by repentance leading to forgiveness and reconciliation. This, and only this, can totally remove the burden of guilt from the sinner. No psychotherapy of any sort can effectively remove true guilt. Only forgiveness by the man who has been wronged or by God who has been sinned against can do this. True guilt is both a legal and theological issue. It is a feeling a man gets when his conscience condemns him. It cannot be analyzed away by a thousand sessions with a psychiatrist. It can be removed instantaneously and permanently once restitution and apology or repentance is followed by forgiveness. If, however, the wrongdoer or sinner is unwilling to repent, his guilt feelings can ultimately lead to anxiety, depression, physical problems, and loss of inner peace. Isaiah said, "But the wicked are like the troubled sea, when it cannot rest, whose waters cast up mire and dirt. There is no peace, saith my God, to the wicked" (Isaiah 57:20–21). Earlier in his prophecy, almost eight hundred years before forgiveness in Christ was understood, Isaiah pleaded: "Come now, and let us reason together, saith the Lord: though your sins be as scarlet, they shall be as white as snow; though they be red like crimson, they shall be as wool" (Isaiah 1:18). Several generations previously, King David of Israel had poured out his soul to God in one of the most beautiful song poems in all of literature: "Bless the Lord, O my soul: and all that is within me, bless his holy name . . . Who forgiveth all thine iniquities; who healeth all thy diseases; . . . The Lord is merciful and gracious, slow to anger and plenteous in mercy. . . . As far as the east is from the west, so far hath he removed our transgressions from us. Like as a father pitieth his children, so the Lord pitieth them that fear him. . . . He knoweth our frame; he remembereth that we are dust. . . . the mercy of the Lord is from everlasting to everlasting. . . ." Read it all. It is Psalms 103.

There are countless references in the New Testament to God's mercy and forgiveness in Christ. Because Christ died on the cross for us we can receive total cleansing from every sin, and this can lead to complete restoration of fellowship with God and man, and to tranquility and peace within. This is the best psychotherapy there is, and it is not magical. Supernatural yes, but magical no. It is divine healing, not comprehended by the sceptical, unmeasurable by human scientific method, but demonstrably effective. John, the apostle of love, said in his first letter: "If we say that we have no sin, we deceive ourselves, and the truth is not in us. If we confess our sins, he is faithful and just to forgive us our sins, and to cleanse us from all unrighteousness" (1 John 1:8–9). Jesus Himself said: "They that are whole have no need of the physician, but they that are sick: I came not to call the righteous, but sinners to repentance" (Mark 2:17).

**False Guilt.**      False guilt is somewhat of a misnomer. It is a useful term because it is short. What it really means, however, is exaggerated or unnecessary guilt. Dr. Paul Tournier, in his well-known book *Guilt and Grace,* writes that false guilt has been described as "functional guilt" and true guilt as "value guilt." He states in his seventh chapter:

> A feeling of "functional guilt" is one which results from social suggestion, fear of taboos or of losing the love of others. A feeling of "value guilt" is the genuine consciousness of having betrayed an authentic standard; it is a free judgment of the self by the self. On this assumption, there is a complete opposition between these two guilt-producing mechanisms, the one acting by social suggestion, the other by moral conviction. . . . "False guilt" is that which comes as a result of the judgments and suggestions of men. "True guilt" is that which results from divine judgment. . . . Therefore real guilt is often something quite different from that which constantly weighs us down, because of our fear of social judgment and the disapproval of men. We become independent of them in proportion as we depend on God.

Freud seemed to see all guilt as false. He denied that guilt was a result of the violation of the moral law of God. It was, rather, the result of too sensitive a superego. Today Christians can see both kinds of guilt. Someone experiencing true guilt resulting from sin needs a Saviour. He who experiences false guilt resulting from sickness needs a physician, specifically a psychiatrist or psychological counselor.

*Causes of false guilt.*   The causes of false guilt stem back to childhood upbringing. Too rigid a superego or conscience can only be developed by too rigid expectations or standards imposed by parents. For example, parents who excessively blame, condemn, judge, and accuse their children when they fail to match up to their expectations cause them to grow up with a warped idea of what appropriate standards are. Unforgiving parents who punish excessively increase guilt. Adequate and proper punishment given in love and with explanation removes guilt. Some parents give too little encouragement, praise, thanks, congratulations, or appreciation. Instead they are never satisfied. However well the child performs in any area of school, play, sports, or social behavior, the parents make him feel they are dissatisfied because he did not do even better. The child sees himself as a constant failure, and he is made to feel guilty because he has failed. He does not realize at his young age what harm his parents are doing to his future feelings of self-worth. He grows up convinced that anything short of perfection is failure. However hard he tries, and even if he actually performs to the maximum that he is capable of, he grows up feeling guilty and inferior.

As an adult he suffers from neurotic or false guilt, low self-esteem, insecurity, and a self-depreciatory pessimistic outlook on all his endeavors and ambitions. He then blames himself and this leads to anger turned inward. He attempts to inflict punishment upon himself because of his feelings of unworthiness. His failures deserve to be judged and punished, and since no one else can do it for him, he punishes himself. This intropunitive retribution, part anger and part hostility, leads inevitably to depression. It can also cause psychosomatic complaints and inappropriate sorts of actions.

*Treatment of false guilt.* False guilt has to be rationalized. It has to be understood and evaluated for what it really is. Complicating feelings such as pride, hostility, and depression have to be separated from the guilt feelings. In particular the Christian patient must understand that self-condemnation is not his prerogative. Only God has the right to judge and condemn. Christians should leave this to Him alone. A thorough investigation of the child-parent relationship has to be pursued in the early part of treatment and the patient helped to see how his false guilt feelings first developed. The patient's own attempts to reduce guilt, if ineffective, should be pointed out to him and dealt with. For example, pretending not to care or indulging in wishful thinking that things will be better next time are very superficial mental avoidance mechanisms which merely cover up the deeper problems. If the patient can be helped to remember some actual experiences when his parents or teachers were excessive in their punishment or condemning in their reaction to a particular incident, these can help him at least partly to understand the origins of his false guilt. If he can be helped to see what true guilt he is experiencing and seek forgiveness from God for this, he will be more easily able to distinguish and get rid of the feelings of false guilt once he has understood them. Unrealistic parental expectations have to be examined in the light of his actual abilities. This will enable him to regain a more wholesome self-concept and feelings of worthiness. It is essential that he then set new goals for himself which are within the limits of his abilities and, for him, realistically attainable. He must not any longer compare his performance with others who are more highly gifted than he is. He should compare his performance with the standard he believes God expects of him, not sinless perfection, but a sincere Christ-honoring endeavor to do God's will in his life as he understands it with the best of his abilities.

*Failure of good works to achieve forgiveness.* Guilt, true or false, is self-destructive and it is, therefore, not God's will for the Christian to suffer from it. A mixture of true and false guilt often leads a Christian to confess the same sin many times. He keeps asking for forgiveness but cannot accept the fact that he only needs to confess once for God to keep His promise of cleansing. Nowhere in the Bible is there any teaching that honest repentance does not immediately lead to full reconciliation with God in Christ. Nowhere are we taught in the Scriptures that we have to do anything in addition to repent to obtain forgiveness. We can never earn it by good works. Failure to understand this basic tenet of Christian doctrine has caused countless Christians to suffer the misery of guilt leading to worry, depression, loss of inner peace, and separation from God.

*Forgiveness brings inner peace.*   Paul told the Philippians that they would have inner peace if they would stop worrying and ask God to deal with all their problems. This was not encouraging them to avoid responsibility. It was assuring them that requests in prayer would bring them what they needed, such as forgiveness to take away guilt for sins committed. "Be careful for nothing; but in everything by prayer and supplication with thanksgiving let your requests be made known unto God. And the peace of God, which passeth all understanding, shall keep your hearts and minds through Christ Jesus" (Philippians 4:6–7). Jesus himself promised: "Peace I leave with you, my peace I give unto you: not as the world giveth, give I unto you. Let not your heart be troubled, neither let it be afraid" (John 14:27).

# 10
# PSYCHOSOMATIC CONDITIONS

**Need for both physical and psychiatric treatment.** In China as long ago as the third millenium B.C. Huang-ti, the Yellow Emperor, wrote that anxiety can cause changes in the body as well as in the mind. These effects are genuine, not just "all in the mind." Real changes take place in various organs which need medical treatment, just as the emotional problems need psychiatric treatment. It is not enough for the physician simply to tell the patient to relax, take it easy or not to worry, and give only physical medications. Also, it is not enough for the psychiatrist to tell him that his nausea or palpitations are merely psychogenic and give him only psychotherapy. The patient needs both treatments: one without the other will be ineffective.

The body can be regarded as a sort of go-between or mediator between the psychological self and the external environment and may therefore become involved in conflicts between them. Sometimes these conflicts can be dealt with by symbolic resolutions, such as in hysterical conversion reactions, by the excessive preoccupation with bodily functions in hypochondriasis, or by a variety of body-image disturbances. Most often, however, resolution is achieved by physical symptoms. This is not hard to understand. A very sad movie or some acute personal disappointment or loss can lead to crying. The production of tears by the lacrimal glands in the eyes, a physical effect, is purely the result of an emotional experience. Suppose however, that for some reason to cry is unacceptable, inappropriate, or unhelpful. Some other organ may become the focus of attention; for example, the stomach. This would cause a stomachache or nausea and vomiting. If this bodily expression continues for long enough, actual structural or anatomic change takes place in the stomach wall and a peptic or gastric ulcer will develop. Henry Maudsley, for whom the psychiatric hospital in London is named, said: "The sorrow which has no vent in tears may make other organs weep."

*Mechanisms of action.* The emotional center in the hypothalamus causes changes to take place in the body by several different physiological mechanisms. The most common are changes in the blood flow through the affected organs, increase or decrease in the amounts of secretion of certain endocrine glands, and changing tone or tension in various skeletal or visceral muscles. The sequence of events is as follows: Psychological or emotional disturbance leads to functional impairment in the particular organ selected (the selection of course is not under the control of the conscious mind). This impairment leads in turn to disease in the actual cells which compose the organ. This process, initially microscopic in its extent, leads ultimately to larger scale (macroscopic) structural alteration in the organ which then produces the particular physiological symptoms and disturbances of which the patient complains.

*Kinds of psychosomatic disorders.* There are essentially two sorts of psychosomatic disorders: those with physical symptoms without organic basis, usually occurring earlier in the disease, and those which develop later with actual organic changes which can be proved by physical examination, laboratory tests, or X-ray. The first sort, in which the doctor would find no demonstrable physical abnormality, includes the following: (1) Upper gastrointestinal symptoms such as nausea, vomiting, indigestion, hyperacidity, stomachache, chronic dyspepsia, and "heartburn." (2)

Lower GI symptoms such as diarrhea, constipation, and vague abdominal pain. (3) Genitourinary symptoms such as urinary frequency, nonspecific urethritis, menstrual disorders, and various sexual problems such as impotence or premature ejaculation in the male, and frigidity, pain on intercourse, or even infertility in the female. (4) General body symptoms such as flushing, sweating, and insomnia. (5) A few specific symptoms such as tension headaches, backaches, cramps, palpitations of the heart, transient shortness of breath, hiccoughs, and attacks of deep breathing called hyperventilation. As can be seen from this long list, it is estimated that almost half the patients seen initially by the family doctor in his general practice have symptoms not based on organic disease but needing either reassurance or psychotherapy.

The second sort includes the following specific disease entities in which definite physical abnormalities can be demonstrated: (1) GI system—chronic gastritis, peptic ulcer, ulcerative colitis, and irritable bowel system; (2) cardiovascular system—high blood pressure, various heart diseases, and migraine which is caused by blood vessel spasms in the head; (3) respiratory system—asthma and hay fever; (4) general body diseases—chronic arthritis, obesity, various skin diseases such as neurodermatosis and pruritus (itching); and (5) a few specific diseases such as some gallbladder troubles, thyroid and other endrocrine gland abnormalities. Even diabetes has some important psychosomatic side effects.

*Psychosomatic personality types.* Personality types tend to predispose to particular psychosomatic ailments. For example, the stomach ulcer patient tends to be the very active, hard living, enthusiastic type of person who is easily upset, nervous or tense, and on edge most of the time. The man with high blood pressure tends to be full of pent-up hostility and aggressive impulses which he is only able to control at the cost of increased tension or anxiety. Sufferers from asthma or hay fever often have conflicts in their interpersonal relationships which stem back to their having received too little or too much mother love with resulting emotional deprivation or overdependence in later life. The diarrhea of colitis is often an expression of nervousness in an anxious person who usually has unconscious resentments, hostilities, and consequent guilt feelings. The patient must be led to understand that his emotional problems make his physical symptoms out of proportion to the actual physical damage.

*Unhelpful misconceptions.* Finally, a warning about misconceptions. Some well-meaning person in attempting to reassure a friend may say, "Just forget about it. It's probably only psychosomatic. You're just imagining you're sick." This is not true. The patient's symptoms are real, not imagined, and they are in need of real treatment, not just an attempt to forget them. Another Job's comforter will say, "Take a few days off. Your aching joints will be fine after a few days in the sun." This is bad advice. A trip to Florida might indeed make the patient improve temporarily but any symptoms of emotional origin will recur until the cause is understood and dealt with. A third fallacy is that "because it's all in the head it can't do you any harm." Tragically, this is very dangerous advice. Many people have died from perforated or bleeding ulcers when earlier treatment could have prevented the situation getting dangerous. Psychosomatic symptoms are real and potentially serious. They need energetic treatment by both a physician and a psychiatrist or counselor.

**Obesity.**     Being overweight is not in itself primarily dangerous to physical health except insofar as it represents an added load on the heart which has to pump blood through all those extra fat capillaries. The things that are dangerous are the factors which caused the obesity in the first place. These are a diet high in calories and fat, and physical inactivity. The poor diet makes the victim more vulnerable to life-threatening diseases such as arteriosclerosis, which is the narrowing of the coronary and other arteries by cholesterol. Inadequate physical activity prevents the body as a whole and especially the heart from building up reserves of energy to protect against unexpected emergency needs.

*Neurotic causes of obesity.* There are of course a few medical causes for obesity such as hormone imbalance and certain metabolic disorders. These need to be fully investigated and treated by a physician. The vast majority of causes, however, are neurotic. Emotional deprivation often leads directly to the practice of eating as a substitute for the needed love and affection. It often starts in the unwanted child or one not given enough mother love. Adolescent girls who are afraid of relationships with the opposite sex allow themselves to get fat as a protection from being dated. They support their self-esteem by believing that all they need to do is lose weight and they will really be very attractive. In fact, however, they are afraid to lose weight because of the deeply suppressed fear that if they did they might find out that after all, they were not so attractive as they thought.

Frustration, poor self-image, hostility, resentment, and depression are all neurotic problems related to a tendency to overeat. To many miserable people the simple fact of eating is the only pleasure they have in life. In excess this is the sin of gluttony. All these factors need to be thoroughly exposed if any psychiatric treatment is going to be successful. Body image and other neurotic disturbances need individual psychotherapy. The obese person who is otherwise relatively well adjusted emotionally sometimes can do well in group therapy. Groups without medical leadership, such as Weight Watchers and TOPS (Take Off Pounds Sensibly), can be very helpful to those people who are strongly motivated to lose weight and do not have complicating psychological or emotional problems.

*Exercise.* Finally don't forget to take plenty of exercise. This applies to everyone, obese or not. Our bodies transform food into energy. Energy that is not used up is stored as body fat. If we eat more than our bodies require for daily activities, we will get overweight. But if we exercise regularly, the excess available calories will be used up and we will not develop fat storage depots around the abdomen and hips. Exercise should not be thought of as something painful done to control weight and keep the body fit. It can also be fun. Calisthenics at home are convenient and burn up 500 unwanted calories per hour if done with sustained effort. By far the best exercise is jogging which is worth 600 and fast running which is worth 900 calories per hour. Handball, squash racquets, basketball, badminton, rowing, cycling, skating, tennis singles, modern dance, swimming, and skiing are all worth between 400 and 600 calories per hour depending on how much you put into it. Golf is good for fresh air but not much good for weight loss. Read *The New Aerobics* by Dr. Kenneth Cooper for practical help in this subject.

Paul said to the Corinthians: "What? know ye not that your body is the temple of the Holy Ghost which is in you, which ye have of God, and ye are not your own? For ye are bought with a price: therefore glorify God in your body, and in your Spirit, which are God's" (1 Corinthians 6:19,20). As Christians we have a duty to God to keep ourselves bodily fit. The Holy Spirit lives in my body as well as in my soul and my responsibility is to take care of both so that God can use me fully without any limitations resulting from my self-destructive neglect.

# 11

# EMOTIONAL PROBLEMS AND RELATED PHYSICAL ILLS

**Common psychosomatic conditions.** There are a few particular problems which are mentioned because they are relatively common and often have psychosomatic overtones. They are headaches, insomnia, the common cold, ulcers, colitis, high blood pressure and heart conditions, arthritis, diabetes, low blood sugar, asthma and the hyperventilation syndrome.

*Headache.* The differential diagnosis of headache would fill several volumes in a neurological library. Physical or organic causes needing neurological rather than psychiatric treatment would include such things as blocked circulation of the cerebrospinal fluid, brain hemorrhage, aneurysm, tumor, or infection (meningitis). Headache can also be caused by such external factors as eyestrain from defective vision, too dull or too glaring light conditions, tight clothing around the neck, poor ventilation, tobacco smoke, and exhaust gases. Hunger, constipation, and menstruation can also cause headaches. Here we are concerned, however, with headaches caused by emotional upsets. These cause increased adrenalin production which leads to increased blood circulation to the brain. This causes the brain to swell, and since it is encased in the rigid, unyielding skull, the increased internal pressure causes the pain of headache. There are two basic types of headaches of emotional origin: migraine headaches and simple tension headaches.

*Migraine headaches,* more common in women, usually occur in high-strung, ambitious, perfectionistic, and driving personalities who are products of rigid conventional families who have high standards and demanding, unforgiving expectations of all members. This leads to suppressed rage because open resistance would threaten the close family attachments. The headaches usually occur in episodes lasting a few hours for a period of several days once every few weeks. Irritability and moodiness usually precede the headaches and occasionally pallor and blurring of vision also occur. The ache itself is usually one-sided and throbs with each heartbeat. Often nausea and vomiting result. Attempts to reduce the cerebral blood flow with Cafergot or similar medications and tranquilization or sedation to calm the patient are the best forms of drug treatment. These need a physician's prescription.

*Tension headaches* can occur in any person irrespective of his tempermental type or family background. They are usually felt on both sides, have no warning signs, do not throb or cause nausea, and are often accompanied by pain in the neck and ache in the shoulders and back. Treatment is usually effective with aspirin though minor tranquilization will also help. If the ache has not disappeared in twenty-four hours, you *must* see a physician to exclude any possible organic cause. Both forms of headaches if frequent and severe enough over a period of time can benefit from psychotherapy. This would help the patient understand his anxiety, hostility, rage, resentment, jealousy, or guilt which has contributed to the changes in cerebral circulation that produced the headaches.

**Insomnia.** Most adults with busy schedules should budget their time to ensure eight hours sleep in every twenty-four. Children and adolescents need nine or ten hours, babies many more. The elderly can do well on six or seven because the pace of life for them is less severe.

Some common causes of insomnia are: (1) discomfort due to noise, light, an uncomfortable bed, physical illness, or extremes of external temperature or humidity; (2) inability to unwind and forget the day's stresses, fears, pressures, apprehensions, or anxiety caused by overwork or worry; (3) depression of mood in any form which can cause difficulty in getting to sleep or staying asleep, or cause early morning waking; (4) guilt, denial, and other protective psychological defense mechanisms which either prevent sleep altogether or repress conscious thoughts into the unconscious mind which then resurrects them in the form of unpleasant dreams and nightmares; and (5) poor physical fitness associated with not enough exercise resulting in inadequate general muscular tiredness and need for rest. Tired mind and muscles guarantee a good night's sleep.

Drug treatment for insomnia should be regarded as an absolute last resort for young people. Adequate physical exercise is usually sufficient for them to ensure good sleep. Middle-aged people need exercise as well but they also need to learn to forget the worries of the day and to relax properly both mentally and muscularly before going to bed. A hot drink and a deep comfortable armchair for half an hour before bed does wonders for many people. Physical illness and emotional causes of insomnia need professional treatment. The elderly should supplement a poor night's sleep with rest periods during the next day. If drugs are unavoidable, such as for the very ill or elderly, try to do without barbiturates. They are addicting, cause morning-after hangovers, and usually necessitate ever increasing doses for continuing effectiveness. Take them only if your family doctor says they are the best for your particular problem. There are effective nonbarbiturate sedatives available.

Remember that forgiveness removes guilt and that committing your worries and fears to God and leaving your burdens at the foot of the cross brings peace to the mind and soul. This inner peace is an essential prerequisite to a good night's sleep. "I will both lay me down in peace, and sleep: for thou, Lord, only makest me to dwell in safety" (Psalms 4:8).

*The Common Cold.*  Although this problem is caused by germs called viruses (not by drafts or getting wet feet), it is mentioned in this chapter because the misery it causes can make one quite depressed and because one's actions and mental attitude toward it can be significant in its prevention and control. A strong, healthy, and fit body kept in fine physical shape always is better equipped to ward off virus infection than one that is overweight, undernourished, overtired, and underexercised. The essentials of maintaining a strong, healthy body are plenty of vigorous exercise and fresh air, a well-rounded and balanced diet, adequate relaxation and sleep, and keeping at least 8–10 feet away from anyone who has a cold.

*Peptic Ulcer.*  Gastric or duodenal ulcers are among the commonest psychosomatic conditions. A recent study of routine postmortem examinations on people who had died from any causes showed evidence of a previous peptic ulcer in 10 percent of them. The "ulcer personality" is usually a man who is very competitive, hard driving, aggressive, determined, and who feels under pressure to succeed. He is frequently anxious, worried, overworked, and often under great emotional strain. He has an internal conflict between an insecure desire to be loved and cared for on the one hand and an adult drive to prove himself to be independent on the other. This conflict leads to guilt and anxiety which cause a chronic increase in the production of adrenalin and of acid in the gastric juice. The increased acid erodes the mucous membrane lining the inside of the stomach wall, and the increased adrenalin reduces the blood supply to it which it needs for adequate defense.

Treatment has to be primarily medical. The hyperacidity has to be reduced by taking alkalis such as Gelusil, Maalox, or other antacids. Surgical removal of the part of the stomach affected may be needed to prevent the dangers of perforation of the ulcer, internal hemorrhage, or the transition of the ulcer into cancer. Psychiatric treatment consists of helping the patient to understand the cause of his conflicts and anxiety and to change his life style to a less stressful routine. In particular his attempts to prove to others his adequacy or superiority and any unworthy motivations in his striving for achievement should be thoroughly investigated and modified. This type of personality problem can be significantly mitigated as a result of a spiritual experience in which the patient can come to yield himself and his ambitions to the will of God and thereby achieve the serenity and inner peace which comes from accepting Christ as Lord in his life.

*Colitis.* Mucous and ulcerative colitis are frequently caused by or made worse by emotional problems. Guilt, hostility, and resentment also sometimes are seen in these patients. Serious episodes of ulcerative colitis often follow a few days or a few weeks after a significant emotional crisis such as a bereavement, divorce, rejection by a loved one, business failure, financial loss, or threat of serious physical illness. Insecurity and loss of self-esteem are sometimes involved. Colitis patients, though usually intelligent and highly sensitive, are often somewhat regressed in their unconscious desire for a protected dependency relationship.

Psychiatric treatment has to be relatively long term. The important element in it should be the assumption of an undemanding, supportive, and even protective parental substitute role by the therapist. The patient, once he feels secure and dependent, will lose or at least reduce his physical symptoms. His other emotional and personality problems can then be dealt with and his self-esteem built up.

*High blood pressure and heart conditions.* Anxiety and prolonged stress tend, through the influence of increased adrenalin and the autonomic (visceral) nervous system, to increase the heart rate, cardiac output, and blood pressure. There are many ways in which the cardiovascular system can be affected by emotional influence. For example, *effort syndrome* or neurocirculatory asthenia is a well-known psychosomatic condition. It is characterized by palpitation, tremors, dizziness, breathlessness, easy fatigability, and headaches. The sufferer cannot tolerate much physical effort. He is afraid it will somehow harm his heart. One of the reasons for this fear is that stress can in fact harm the heart if excessive or protracted. Tests done over twenty years ago proved conclusively that the time taken for blood to clot is much reduced in people living under stress. Obviously some, as yet unknown, chemical in the blood is making it more likely to coagulate than in people not under stress. Stress, therefore, increases the chances of a clot or thrombus developing in the coronary artery which supplies the heart itself. *Coronary artery thrombosis, angina pectoris,* and *myocardial infarction* are all terms used to describe a heart attack. The angina is the tight binding pain across the front of the chest associated with the thrombosis, and the infarction is the permanent damage done to the heart muscle. Although a narrowed artery has to be present for the heart attack to take place, stress which leads to strong emotional changes contributes to its development.

The precise mechanism by which this occurs is not fully understood, but it is well known that the *coronary type,* like the ulcer patient, is a hard-driving, ambitious, competitive man who allows himself little time for relaxation. He very often is overweight, physically unfit, and a heavy smoker. The stress in his life puts an unyielding strain on his heart. High cholesterol in his blood from too much fat in his diet and too little physical exercise prepare the way for the attack which can come any time that the heart has to exert itself unexpectedly either in an unusual physical effort or even merely in a moment of emotional excitement. Psychiatric treatment either before or after the attack or both must be aimed toward helping the patient to reduce his driving life style and to accept a less stressful daily routine. Apprehensions of death must be allayed whenever present.

*High blood pressure* can be caused by diseases of the kidneys, adrenals, or central nervous system which result in narrowing of the arteries. The narrowing forces the heart to pump more strongly to push the blood through them because peripheral resistance is increased. Emotional tension, as previously described, mediated through the autonomic nervous system can cause constriction of the peripheral arteries. Inability to express and discharge suppressed rage or hostility builds up an inner tension which can lead to this destructive mechanism. Hypertensive personalities often seem outwardly to be affable and friendly, even serene, but this facade usually hides strong conflicting emotions of hostility and dependency toward authority figures. In addition to treatment with drugs to lower the blood pressure, psychotherapy is often essential to allow expression of hostility by the patient and to enable him to understand the significance of stress in his life as a causative factor in his disease. Worry, anxiety, and fear are common in our generation. Stresses are great especially in today's pressures of urban living. We are living in the end times in which "men's hearts [are] failing them for fear" (Luke 21:26) and which presage the return of the Lord of Glory.

*Arthritis.* Rheumatoid arthritis is mentioned here because of the well-known fact that either the original onset or an exacerbation (worsening) of the condition often follows or is related to a period of emotional stress. The patients are of course constitutionally predisposed to the condition. It tends to run in families. The same sorts of emotional and physical stresses previously described which can cause ulcers or colitis in some people, heart and blood pressure problems in others can cause arthritis in those with this inherited genetic tendency. The sufferer is often outwardly composed and friendly, tries to be helpful to others rather than dependent and tries not to complain or express his feelings. Underneath, however, is often intense hostility and resentment, usually directed toward his closest relatives. Arthritics frequently seem to come from families in which there is a domineering mother and a passive father. Death of the mother is a very common precipitating event in younger patients. Separation or divorce or other serious personal disappointments during middle age can have the same effect. Conflicting feelings of guilt and resentment which he is unable to express verbally lead to the degenerative process in the joints.

Treatment is both medical and psychiatric. The internist has a wide variety of medications to try including aspirin, cortisone or other steroids, and gold injections. Occupational and physical therapy may be needed for severe disability. Psychotherapy has to be mainly supportive with encouragement to remain as active as possible. Resentment and guilt need to be expressed, and in this way the patient can not only feel better but he can reduce the frequency and severity of the exacerbations. Actual damage done to the joints is, however, irreversible. Therapy must also, therefore, aim at helping the patient learn to live as efficiently and happily as possible within his physical limitations.

*Diabetes.*    Diabetes mellitus is a condition in which the pancreas produces too little insulin. This causes a rise in the concentration of sugar in the blood, a condition known as hyperglycemia. This is a dangerous disease which killed millions of people before insulin was discovered and made available in synthetic form in the 1920s. Diabetics who take insulin or a chemical equivalent and also control their diet and energy output can now live quite safely. However, some of them with personal emotional problems have difficulty adhering to a strict regimen. Periods of stress resulting in increased adrenalin circulation leads to increased release of sugar from the liver into the blood. This upsets the glucose-insulin balance in the patient. The glucose tolerance test, the best way to measure this balance, is known to show higher blood sugar levels if the patient is feeling angry, hostile, or anxious than if he is feeling accepted and at peace within himself.

Crisis or stress not only affects the actual glucose level in the blood but it also may affect the daily routine of accurate intakes of food and insulin. Most of the uncontrolled complications of diabetes, such as disruption of the electrolyte (salt) balance and coma, occur after some emotional crisis. Seriously depressed or suicidal diabetics occasionally may deliberately neglect their insulin injections or pills as a gesture of hopelessness. Children with diabetes are especially difficult to manage because reward and punishment systems in the family often revolve around eating, parties, treats, and gifts. "Brittle" diabetics, those whose blood sugar levels are difficult to keep under control, need psychotherapy in addition to supervision by an internist. Causes of emotional stress need to be talked through, hostility has to be verbally expressed, and feelings of hopelessness dispelled by support and encouragement.

*Low Blood Sugar.* This condition is the exact opposite of diabetes. There is too much insulin and too little glucose circulating in the blood. These conditions are known as hyperinsulinism and hypoglycemia respectively and are essentially synonymous. They are very common and occur for brief periods in almost everyone from time to time. The significance of low blood sugar is that it can cause temporary emotional upsets such as easy irritability, lack of concentration, a don't-care attitude, or generalized mental and physical fatigue. Every wife knows that the time to ask her husband for money is after she has given him his supper. She is much more likely to get what she wants when his blood sugar, low from his day's work and trip home, has been elevated by the protein, fat, and carbohydrate in his meal. For the same reason, it is not wise to go forth in the morning to face the day's activities without an adequate breakfast. Just a cup of coffee is not enough to take in between last night's supper and midday lunch. Performance during the morning and certainly interpersonal relationships will be far more efficient and pleasant if blood sugar level is not too low.

Insulin works in the cells all over the body helping them to use up glucose which is the essential source of heat and energy. The brain especially needs a plentiful supply of both glucose and insulin in the right proportions for its healthy functioning. So does the heart. Deprivation of these will cause the brain to produce feelings of fatigue and irritability.

*Hyperventilation Syndrome.* This is a common respiratory psychosomatic ailment. It consists of episodes of overbreathing by someone having an anxiety attack. The patient often does not realize that he is overbreathing, but if it lasts a long time (several minutes), he tends to build up too much oxygen and lose too much carbon dioxide from his blood which causes a chemical imbalance. This leads to symptoms such as sweating, giddyness, unsteady gait, and pain in the chest. As anxiety increases, the patient gets a paradoxical sensation of air hunger or shortness of breath which causes even more gasping for air. Eventually he will faint and his temporary loss of consciousness enables his respiration rate to return to normal. Treatment consists of tranquilization by both explanatory and supportive psychotherapy and by medications, by injections if need be in emergency.

*Asthma.*   Asthma and hay fever are usually considered to be primarily allergic respiratory conditions. Any allergy, however, has some psychosomatic overtones in that the subjective response of the patient is sometimes out of proportion to the cause. In an asthmatic attack the small tubes through which the air enters the lungs go into spasm which constricts them so much that breathing becomes frighteningly difficult. Even if an allergy caused the constriction in the first place, the anxiety which naturally follows can make the situation worse unless the victim can relax.

About 400 B.C. Hippocrates taught that there was a definite connection between emotional arousal and the precipitation of an asthmatic attack. A recent survey involving extensive review of medical literature reveals that perhaps as many as 75 percent of all asthmatic attacks are set off by emotional rather than allergenic factors. There seems to be an asthmatic personality type. He is usually anxious, easily irritated, submissive, lacking in self-confidence, and often maternally dependent with conflicting repressed hostility.

Asthma is common in children and is often made worse by overanxious mothers. It tends to improve in adolescence and adult life unless there is both an allergic and a personality predisposition to it. Tension in the child's home can make him develop asthma, as evidenced by the spontaneous improvement when he goes away from his parents to summer camp. Domineering, overprotective mothers and passive fathers tend to increase the likelihood of asthma in sensitive children, especially if they cannot feel the security of genuine overtly demonstrated affection and love. An asthmatic attack in either children or adults gives the patient two immediate gains. First, he avoids responsibility for dealing with whatever was the threatening or frustrating situation which sparked the attack, and second, he gains attention and sympathy from those around him, which gives him some emotional satisfaction. Both these gains must be thoroughly explored if any psychotherapy is going to be successful.

Therapy should also be concerned with defining the emotionally disturbing situations which start off the attacks. It should also help the patient see the connection and then become willing to change or at least to control his type of response. Underlying insecurity and dependency needs should be resolved, and in the case of children, the parents need to be educated to understand their role in the situation. Treatment however is primarily medical. Adrenalin available in a spray to inhale is the most quickly effective agent. This usually can be supplemented by injections. Steroids and tranquilizers may be helpful in calming and controlling once the acute attack has passed.

# 12
# PROFESSIONAL HELP: WHEN IT IS NEEDED AND HOW TO GET IT

**Universality of emotional illness.**    So often the first reaction by the Christian to realizing that something is wrong is to have the attitude: "I shouldn't have emotional problems. I'm a Christian. If I'm emotionally upset, it must be because I am not in a right relationship with Christ. There must be some unconfessed sin in my life." Notice the confused thinking here. First, it is absolutely untrue that Christians cannot or should not become mentally ill. We are just as vulnerable as pagans. It is true, however, that we have God's healing power available; but this healing power may include human help when God makes it available. Second, it is completely wrong theologically to think that suffering is necessarily the direct result of sin. It may be so occasionally. Sometimes our own folly can indeed lead to results that are painful, but generally I have not found in my experience that God punishes Christians by inflicting mental illness upon them. He is a God of righteousness and justice but not vindictiveness. Suffering may be part of God's permissive will, allowed temporarily for the purpose of yielding a greater blessing later. I do not believe it is ever to be seen as executive punishment.

*Share problems with a friend.*   What, then, should the Christian do when he gets to the point where his personal problems are beginning to cause him significant emotional distress or when his functioning in any area of life is being adversely affected by them? First, let him admit it and get help. This is not denying his faith but recognizing his need. It is facing reality and appropriating to himself God's provision of human help. He should share his problems with someone he trusts, preferably a more mature Christian of the same sex. This person must be willing to be a good listener and to spend time and expend effort in really caring for his brother in need. There is not enough of this caring in our churches. We are all in such a rush to be about our own business, stuck in our own little narrow ruts, with a limited vision of the crying human need around us. We magnanimously give one hundred dollars for foreign mission work or the new organ fund but resent spending a few minutes patiently listening to a friend who is desperate to tell his troubles to someone he believes cares. This is the key to good psychotherapy and counseling—to care, to really care, and to let the sufferer know that you care. If more Christians made themselves available in this way to help the weaker brother and sister in need when the troubles first started, there would be far fewer numbers of them having to go later for professional help. The burden of my message is that caring Christians can significantly contribute to the mental and emotional health of their fellow church members and Christian friends. To do so we must make ourselves available and give time and our own emotional energies and resources to succor those in need. We do this by listening and caring. Be patient in listening even if you are in a hurry to do something else. Care by allowing the sufferer to share his burden with you. Give him the gift of your time and genuine sympathy.

**When professional help is indicated.**    What if the problems are more serious and a caring Christian friend really cannot help? What are the indications for professional help? If you have read this book up to this point, you will know what are the major psychiatric disease categories, but what is more important is that you should be able to recognize at what point you should tell your friend that he needs more help—professional help—than you can give him by sharing his burden. The two key points to consider are *functioning and feeling.* The main points are elaborated on in chapter 3 and the characteristics of mental health are described. Consider your friend in the light of how well he is able to function in those categories and also how he is feeling. Does he or anyone close to him think that his effectiveness in any area of functioning is impaired? Does he feel anxious or depressed or have any other distressing emotions? Does he have any of the symptoms mentioned in the later descriptive chapters? If the answer to any of these questions is yes, the probability is that your friend needs professional help. Consider also the duration of the problems. If they occurred only recently, there is always the possibility that they are only temporary and will soon resolve themselves and not recur. But if the duration has been a matter of months or years without relief from any self-help measures, something more should be sought. If, in spite of earnest prayer and supplication that the problem would disappear, it has not done so, the time has come to use the human help that God has provided. What then should the Christian do?

*Pastor will help find a therapist.*   Most church members go first to their minister or priest. He is usually able to recognize quickly if the problems are of a spiritual nature, in which case he can give pastoral counseling, which is especially valuable in helping those who are suffering from guilt, loss of assurance, or any situation which affects the believer's relationship to God in Christ. But if the pastor feels that the problems are not responsive to prayer and spiritual help and are severe enough to warrant specially trained professional help, he will refer the sufferer to a clinical psychologist or psychiatrist. These men or women are skilled in treating severe problems such as depression, anxiety, personality disorders, or serious situational adjustment reactions. If the patient is ill enough to need medications, hospitalization, or shock treatment, he should be referred to a psychiatrist, who is a medical doctor as well as a psychotherapist.

*The non-Christian doctor.* It is often at this point that the Christian resists further treatment insisting that he will only go to a psychiatrist who is known to be a believing Christian. He is afraid that a non-Christian psychiatrist will try to destroy or ridicule his personal faith or try to talk him out of it. At the very least, he feels, the therapist won't understand his particular problems if the therapist is not himself a believer. I think it is essential to emphasize, however, that this is not always true. Especially if the problems are sufficiently serious to require medications or hospitalization, the doctor treating them, at least initially, does not have to be a fully understanding, believing Christian. Just as it is not vital that the surgeon who mends the Christian's broken leg be himself a devout follower of Christ, so it is in the case with the psychiatrist. It is good if he is, but in the treatment of *serious* psychiatric illness it is not essential. What is important is that he gives the best medications on the market and does his best to help the patient with psychotherapy, in the hospital if need be.

Secondly, in defence of my professional colleagues, I can testify from my knowledge of many of them over a period of several years that the vast majority of them, even if not believers themselves, generally do have respect for another person's religious faith. This is especially so if that faith represents one of the patient's strengths. It is not true that most psychiatrists are atheists. Obviously some are, but the majority would call themselves agnostics. Generally they would encourage a person in his personal religious faith if they could see that it was of such quality as to be a stabilizing influence in his life. They will concentrate in therapy in dealing with the causes of the mental illness which most often, especially in the psychoses, are unrelated to the patient's personal religious beliefs. Religious belief will usually be discussed only if the psychiatrist feels, after he has gotten to know the patient well, that the patient is using his religion to avoid responsibility or facing reality. Remember that nothing will be revealed in therapy which is not already fully known to God. He understands us to the very depths. Through psychotherapy we can perhaps learn to understand ourselves better, and this can lead to a deeper and stronger faith. A Christian who has a strong, well-established personal faith needs not fear conventional psychotherapy. It is not a technique for destroying faith. It is intended to help straighten out the psychological disorders which are preventing the Christian from enjoying the abundant life that faith provides.

*When a Christian therapist is preferable.*   However, if the patient's emotional problems are inextricably bound up with his beliefs, then a Christian psychiatrist or counselor is desirable or sometimes essential. For example, I recently saw in my office a man who was suffering from deep-seated guilt feelings leading to depression which necessitated large doses of medications and a brief stay in the hospital. He felt he had lost his eternal salvation because of unforgivable sin. In addition to giving him medical treatment, I was eventually able to help him unravel the confusion in his mind about his relationship with his earthly father who had been a very demanding and unforgiving tyrant and who had made him feel inferior and unworthy. He had carried this memory over into his concept of his heavenly Father whom he saw as unaccepting and condemning. He could not believe that forgiveness was a free gift from God. Emotionally he could not accept that his sins were forgivable. When he finally saw consciously his erroneous, unconscious comparison between his earthly and heavenly fathers, he became less guilty and depressed. Eventually he did not need medication and was able to return to work and to his family with peace of mind and restored fellowship with his Lord.

*Christian factors in therapy.*   The actual psychotherapy I had given him was not significantly different from that which he would have gotten from a non-Christian psychiatrist. However, there were three factors which were different. First, he felt more easily able to express his problems in Biblical terms and knew that I understood what he was trying to say. Second, being assured that I was myself a committed Christian believer, he was much more readily able to accept my explanations and respond to my suggestions. Third, I was able to read a few relevant passages of Scripture to him and we often concluded our sessions with prayer together. My prayers invoking the healing power of the Holy Spirit, I am certain, were a major contributing factor in his recovery.

**Areas of professional help.**   How does a Christian find professional help for emotional problems? His family doctor or his pastor would certainly be able to help him find a nearby psychiatrist, psychologist, marriage counselor, local hospital psychiatric outpatient department, or low-cost clinic for psychotherapy.

*Psychiatrists.*   Be sure, if you want to go privately, that you find someone who is properly qualified. A psychiatrist has an M.D. degree. He is a medical doctor as well as a fully trained psychotherapist. He has had a minimum of twelve years of full-time training beyond high school. He has not only been to college and medical school but has also done a year of internship and not less than three years of special training, called a residency, in mental hospitals and psychiatric clinics. He can go still further if he wishes. He can do several more years of part-time study including a personal analysis to become a psychoanalyst, and not less than two years after his residency he can take an exam to become a diplomate of the American Board of Psychiatry and Neurology. Qualifications and requirements in most foreign countries are essentially the same nowadays. If there is any doubt in your mind about your psychiatrist's qualifications, it is perfectly legitimate to ask him if he is a diplomate of the American Board of Psychiatry and Neurology, if he is a member of either the American Psychiatric or American Psychoanalytic Association, or if he is a member of the American Medical Association. If necessary, you are entitled to write to find out. A psychiatrist has no obligation to join any of these, however, and he may be fully qualified without having done so. Nevertheless, at the very least, by law, he must have a license to practice medicine in his state, and his credentials are often prominently displayed in his office or waiting room.

What about the practical question of the actual *availability of psychiatrists?* In 1971, with the population of the United States approximately 210 million, there were about twenty thousand members of the American Psychiatric Association, about one-tenth of them being also trained as psychoanalysts. There were about another eight to ten thousand psychiatrists who were not members of the A.P.A. This represents a distribution of one psychiatrist to every seven thousand people. In view of the great need, this is woefully inadequate, and yet it is the highest proportion of any country in the world except Israel. Another serious problem is the maldistribution of psychiatrists. More than half work in the fifteen largest cities in the country, and again more than half are in the five states of California, Massachusetts, Illinois, Pennsylvania, and New York. About 15 percent of all A.P.A. members are in California, the vast majority in San Francisco or Los Angeles. Almost 20 percent are in New York City alone, a third of these having their offices in the upper East Side of Manhattan. There are more psychiatrists in the 30-block area between

East 60th and East 90th Streets than there are in any other state of the Union except California and any other country except the Soviet Union. In spite of these startling figures, however, the psychiatrists there are very busy. Almost all of them are fully booked with their available time completely filled within a few months of starting in practice. Also the low-cost clinics and hospital outpatient departments to which many of them donate several hours per week without pay are loaded to full capacity, with waiting lists sometimes extending to several months.

*Clinical psychologists.* In addition to M.D.'s there is another group which is entitled to practice psychotherapy. They are clinical psychologists with a Ph.D. degree who have specialized in psychotherapy. Some have gone further and had psychoanalytic training as well. They are called lay analysts. Both these are usually members of the American Psychological Association. They also have to have a state license. They may practice individual or group psychotherapy, but they may not prescribe medications, give shock treatment, or treat patients in hospitals except under the supervision of a physician. Although there are several thousand psychologists, only a few of them are trained for actual patient counseling or therapy. The majority are involved in business, industry, administration, research, teaching, or psychological testing. This last is usually requested by the psychiatrist as part of his initial evaluation of a new patient. Psychological tests can help him to arrive at a definite diagnosis and decide whether the problem is purely psychological or partly organic in origin. Personality structure, the patient's potential for treatment, and level of intellectual functioning can be measured.

*Social workers.* A psychiatric social worker who has a Master of Social Work degree, can also be trained to practice psychotherapy under a doctor's supervision and would be accredited by the Academy of Certified Social Workers. She is also trained to act as a liaison between the medical team and the patient's family. She can help the family to understand the patient's illness and where necessary would visit homes to evaluate and advise on conditions when relevant to mental health and general welfare.

*Other therapists.*   The rest of the supply of psychotherapists consists of psychologists and psychiatrists still in training, psychiatric nurses, marriage guidance counselors, and rabbis, priests, and ministers struggling to provide psychotherapy in addition to spiritual guidance for their parishioners. Of these last, however, the Academy of Religion and Mental Health estimates that fewer than 10 percent have adequate knowledge of psychiatry. Their courses in seminary were for the most part limited to pastoral counseling without training in how to recognize those less serious aspects of mental illness which they could deal with themselves if properly taught.

*Avoid the unqualified.*   Beware of going to someone who advertises himself simply as a "psychotherapist" or "psychoanalyst" whether it be in a phone book listing, on a calling card, in a newspaper or magazine, or on his office door. If he does not have an M.D. or Ph.D. degree, check his credentials very carefully. There is a greater number of quacks and charlatans claiming to help people with emotional problems than in any other health field. The National Association for Mental Health, Inc., and the Family Service Association of America in New York City will both give you information on how and where to get treatment either privately or in a low-cost clinic or local hospital.

**Cost of treatment.**     What of the cost of treatment? A private psychiatrist's fee varies from $20 to $50 per 45-minute session. A six-months course of treatment with weekly sessions could, therefore, cost from $500 to $1,250. Although these figures sound high, one should consider them in terms of what can be achieved. If suffering is relieved, one's life style improved, and good interpersonal relationships restored as a result, surely this is worth one-third of what is paid for the average family car? Psychoanalysis, as distinct from "regular" psychotherapy, usually necessitates several visits per week and lasts three to five years. It is slow but very thorough in terms of gaining self-understanding. It may cost considerably in excess of $30,000. Even this enormous sum is considered worth it by those who have been able to afford to go through it. However, my personal prediction is that, because of the time and expense involved, private psychoanalysis as a therapeutic technique will gradually decline and die but that the theoretic principles of psychoanalysis will continue to be taught as a medical discipline until something better is discovered or invented to explain and treat emotional and personality problems.

*Clinics.*  Most low-cost clinics and hospital psychiatric outpatient departments charge less than $20 per session, the actual fee usually being set after a social worker has evaluated the family income and resources. Presently Medicare pays 80 percent of psychiatric treatment for those over sixty-five. Medicaid pays the total bill for those on welfare, but since the amount is much less than a regular private fee, there are few psychiatrists who accept Medicaid patients. The relative scarcity of psychiatrists has forced more and more general family doctors to take on more of the responsibility of psychotherapy. This is basically a good idea anyway if they can find the time to do it. Many patients who go to a psychiatrist could be treated just as well by a regular physician if he will devote the time.

**Information about Christian therapists.**    If you are looking for definitely Christian-oriented treatment, the Christian Medical Society, the Christian Association for Psychological Studies, and the Fuller Theological Seminary Graduate School of Psychology may be able to give you local information if they have it available.

Try also your own pastor or any local Christian physician. Either of them should know of any Christian psychiatrist or counselor in your area. A nearby Christian college with a department of psychology will probably have some helpful local information. The best source of information, however, is the Narramore Christian Foundation in Rosemead, California. For over twenty years its staff has been helping Christians all over the country to find help for emotional illnesses and family problems. Their extensive literature distribution and Dr. Narramore's regular radio broadcasts all over the world have been a source of help to millions.

# 13
# THEORIES AND TECHNIQUES OF PSYCHOLOGICAL TREATMENT

**Variety of theories.**    In this chapter some of the basic principles of psychotherapy in general use today are described. Psychiatry is still in its infancy as far as its development as a science or art is concerned, and therefore there is much disagreement over psychiatric theories and techniques among different schools of thought. In practice however many different types of psychotherapy have been demonstrated to work effectively in carefully preselected cases. In spite of a lack of established methodology a great deal is being accomplished both in alleviating mental suffering and in helping patients to function more effectively.

Most psychiatric conditions and personality problems have taken several years to develop and so it is not surprising that treatment takes time. Understanding of personality structure, thought patterns, mood and behavior characteristics, and emotional conflicts and problems cannot be done quickly. Psychotherapy is usually a long process requiring patience and perseverance on the part of both the doctor and the patient.

**Psychotherapeutic procedure.**    Psychotherapy means treatment of the mind and describes verbal techniques used by a psychiatrist in his dialogue with his patients. There is nothing magical about it, and it is important for patients to understand from the beginning that hard work is involved both by themselves and by the therapist. It is essential for success that the patient desire help and is motivated to persist in treatment for the purpose of obtaining it. Before any progress can be made, however, several important things have to be done in preparation.

First, the doctor has to acquire a thorough understanding of the patient as a person, his personality structure, what his family background and upbringing was like, what his present life circumstances are at home, at work, and in society, what his present problems are and how they developed, and why he came to get help at this particular time. This is why he needs to take an extensive initial history during the first few sessions. This consists of a thorough description by the patient of his problems as he understands them so far. It includes a list of symptoms and any possible causes or situational factors which precipitated them. He should carefully describe their onset, duration, intensity, frequency, and what makes them worse or better. He should give a personal biographical sketch summarizing his main experiences in family, school, college, military, job or career, and social pursuits. Previous physical and mental history, sex life, religious beliefs, personal relationships, goals, and ambitions are all revealed for the therapist to obtain an overall picture of the person he is trying to help.

Next, the psychiatrist must do a thorough mental examination by asking some special questions and observing reactions. He will try to evaluate the patient's appearance, emotional reactions, mood, attitude, and the spontaneity, rate, and continuity of his speech. His thought processes are evaluated as to content, logical sequence, reality content, keeping to the point, orientation, memory, judgment, and insight. Sometimes special psychological tests are helpful.

Third, he will need to postulate a provisional diagnosis as a base line for treatment, even if this has to be changed as he gets to know the patient better. The causes and dynamics of the patient's disorder must be understood in order to establish a corrected diagnosis later. He will then discuss very thoroughly with the patient what are the realistic goals of treatment so that from the outset they are working together toward the same agreed objective. The most frequent goals are the removal of painful symptoms, translating insight and understanding into appropriate action, and the altering of patterns of behavior so that future stresses can be handled more successfully than previously. Unrealistic expectations and misconceptions on the part of the patient must be straightened out as early as possible to avoid later disappointments and loss of confidence in the doctor. Poor motivation for therapy, inability to accept the fact that he can be helped, refusal to accept the therapist's opinion as to his need, and feelings of hostility, excessive dependency, or sexual attraction toward him have to be dealt with before progress can be made.

*Qualities of a good therapist.* A good working relationship must be developed between doctor and patient as soon as possible. The doctor on his part will develop a genuine interest in the patient and a desire to help him. He must communicate early in treatment that he understands, accepts and sympathizes with his patient. Also, he should extend warmth and not show irritability, impatience, or boredom even if he feels them. His worst mistake would be to let the patient ever feel that he was not interested or that he did not really care. He must make himself available at all times even if this involves some invasion of his privacy.

A successful therapist must be a properly trained and experienced observer of human behavior. He must be sufficiently secure in his own identity and personal value system not to be threatened by any patient he takes on for treatment. He should be able to listen patiently, be nonjudgmental and then articulate clearly what he understands to be the patient's problems and his answers to them. He must be confident within himself that he can help the patient and then radiate this confidence across to him so that the patient can gradually develop confidence in himself. Although the therapist is usually brighter intellectually and better educated than the patient, when this is not the case it is essential to success in therapy that this fact in no way affects the confidence of the patient in his doctor.

*Transference.* The patient should develop a trust in his doctor and believe that he is sincerely doing his best, that he understands his suffering, and that he is capable of helping him. This trust often develops into a deep affection, and realizing this, the doctor can use the patient's emotional involvement as a helpful, additional resource in the whole therapeutic process. By the very nature of the relationship, however, the patient often unconsciously identifies the therapist with one of his parents and therefore transfers to him some of the emotions and attitudes he formerly had in relation to this person. This phenomenon is known as transference and may be either positive or negative depending on whether the former relationship was friendly and loving or fearful and hating.

*Countertransference.* The therapist also develops toward the patient positive or negative emotions known as countertransference. Handling the transference-countertransference situation so as to use it to help rather than hinder treatment is a very important part of therapy. For example, the patient should feel able to ventilate his anger and hostility at or to his therapist without fear of being rejected by him for it. He can then learn a new style of emotional response to stressful situations and thereby suffer less when the situations arise in his life outside. For the patient thoroughly to learn how to adapt to emotional pain, or change his behavioral response to it, he must understand the environmental stresses that cause it, his own emotional structure and limitations, and his previously inadequate responses that failed to avoid it. Psychotherapy in essence is his learning better ways to respond successfully to pain of any origin.

Remember that psychotherapy is also a relationship. It is a patient-therapist relationship brought about for the purpose of effecting change in the patient. It is past, present, and future. The patient must understand and interpret his past behavior, develop insight into his present situation, and reeducate his emotions, goals, and values toward a future productive and adjusted life. Free and uninhibited full expression of the patient's thoughts and feelings, so essential to success in treatment, is only possible if the patient-doctor relationship becomes and remains one of mutual trust, respect, and even affection.

*Psychotherapeutic objectives.*   Later therapeutic tasks include exploring environmental frustrations and interpersonal conflicts which lead to anxiety or withdrawal. Guilt needs to be exposed and dealt with. Unwillingness or inability to master anxiety has to be evaluated and corrected. Incentive and motivation for change has to be created. Remediable environmental stresses have to be changed and irremediable ones avoided or accepted. Painful symptoms of any sort which affect efficient functioning must be eliminated, even at the cost of other symptoms arising so long as they are less debilitating. Toward the end of treatment the patient must be helped to abandon primary and secondary neurotic gains and stop resisting return to normalcy and self-dependence. He should by then be able to make his own decisions, to establish his own values and goals, to be assertive and independent and be both functioning efficiently and feeling free of anxiety or depression. If finally it is agreed by the therapist, the patient, his immediate family, his friends, and fellow workers that his present feelings, behavior, and functioning are acceptable to all concerned, he is ready to terminate treatment. This is a high standard, rarely fully attained, but it represents a definite goal to strive for.

The therapist on his part must neither probe too deeply and quickly at the start nor avoid those issues which make him feel anxious himself. He should never be impatient at the patient's resistance but discuss this openly. He should not become frustrated at the patient's slow progress or push him too hard or too fast toward their agreed objectives and goals. He must balance directive and nondirective techniques in accordance, not with his theories, but with the particular patient's needs. At the end of treatment he must strictly avoid any overprotective or dominating attitude and must encourage independence. He should tell the patient at their last meeting that he should feel free to call him at any time either for more treatment or simply to keep in touch. I have several ex-patients who are doing well and who occasionally call me at home in the evening just for a five-minute chat to let me know how they are doing. It is like fresh contacts with old friends which provide both them and me with feelings of satisfaction and affection.

**Basic approaches to therapy.**     There are many different types of psychotherapy and many different schools of psychological theory, but basic to all of them is the fact that all behavior is directed toward a goal, even if the patient does not consciously realize it, and that behavior is a learned response, usually developed during the early years of life. Many of these responses have to be unlearned, and the patient reeducated to new ways of reacting to his real life problems. The techniques by which this is achieved are as many as the number of therapists, and experimental studies comparing one type of technique with another usually show that they produce similar results. There are three basic approaches, one concerned with analysis and interpretation of behavior, another with offering support and encouragement, and the third being definitely directive.

*Psychoanalysis.*     The first basic approach to therapy, the interpretive, is known as psychoanalysis and was first developed by Sigmund Freud. In this technique the patient goes three, four, or even five times per week and lies on a couch with his analyst seated behind him so that there is no distracting eye-to-eye contact. The patient then reports his thoughts, experiences, feelings, and dreams as they come to his mind, the analyst being a passive listener at least initially. This is known as free-association. The transference relationship that develops between them is fully discussed together with related emotional problems, such as resistance to treatment, which are typical of the patient's distorted relationships with other people. Unconscious content and conflicts are brought to conscious awareness so that the patient gains insight into his need for change in his personality structure.

The basic theory is that all behavior is predetermined by previous experiences and is directed toward a purpose which might not be consciously realized. Conflicts involving the id, ego, and superego (see chapter 9) which caused frustrations in basic sexual and aggressive instincts are exposed and better methods of adaptation or change are discussed. This process can take many years because established behavior patterns resist change. A complete analysis would rarely take less than three hundred sessions, five hundred to eight hundred or more being the usual. Only the wealthy few can enjoy it and the analyst can treat only a dozen or so patients per week. It is therefore very uneconomical in consideration of the shortage of trained doctors. The most suitable patients for this type of treatment are young or middle-aged men or women who have mild neurotic personality or situational adjustment problems, no psychotic thought processes or severe character disorders, but plenty of time and money.

The *neo-Freudian school,* conisting of people like Adler, Sullivan, Rado, and Horney, has modified Freudian technique to make it shorter and less intense. The psychobiological theory of Adolf Meyer consists of distributive analysis and synthesis of conscious rather than unconscious material. Actual problems are discussed as in ordinary conversation, and by the process of inductive reasoning, the therapist helps the patient modify emotional reactions and behavior patterns. Psychotherapy, using some but not all psychoanalytic principles, has given the technique greater flexibility of use so that more people can be treated less expensively. This is probably the most widely used form of psychotherapy in the United States today.

*Supportive treatment.* The second basic approach to psychotherapy, supportive or suppressive treatment, is usually temporary and is used where strengthening rather than changing of defense mechanisms is needed. It is an especially valuable technique in the elderly, in a temporary reactive depression, in some chronic anxiety states, in the borderline psychotic, and as an adjunct to drug or shock treatment. The goals are limited to restoring previously adequate adjustments temporarily disrupted by the patient's sickness, and to preventing the more serious emotional collapse called decompensation. Later, after regaining stability, defenses can be changed when he is willing and strong enough to tolerate it. Recent reality is faced up to and reassurance, advice, suggestion, reasoning, encouragement, and even persuasion are used where they are appropriate. The use of authority and a permissive attitude to relieve guilt are carefully balanced. The basic aims are to dispel anxiety and reconstruct hope, but the therapist must be careful not to allow the patient to regress into passivity and become helplessly dependent on him.

*Directive therapies.* Thirdly, the directive therapies have been gaining widespread acceptance in the last few years because of the length, expense, and frequent failure of analytic methods. *Behavior or conditioning therapy,* developed from the conditioned reflex experiments of Pavlov, has the basic premise that since all behavior is learned, if the original learning experiences can be extinguished, and new ones put in their place, behavior can be changed. Change can be produced by giving the patient either a reward of some pleasurable gratification to reinforce the desire for new behavior patterns, or some form of punishment or pain to help discourage any reversion to the previous undesirable behavior. This technique of reward and punishment is called positive and negative reinforcement. Aversion treatment with apomorphine injections to make sexual perverts vomit when shown pictures of their desired sexual objects is such an example. Antabus treatment for alcoholics is another.

*Reality therapy,* recently popularized by William Glasser, stresses responsibility as the basic quality of mental health and reciprocal involvement between doctor and patient as a necessary prerequisite to successful treatment. More than any other therapeutic technique or theory that I have studied, the principles of reality therapy, I have found, is the best for my type of Christian practice. In chapter 14 I elaborate some of the ways I have tried to integrate them into my Bible-centered therapy and counseling efforts.

*Marital therapy* with both marriage partners and *family therapy* with their children as well are becoming increasingly used. Marriage problems are impossible to help unless both partners desire improvement in their marital relationship and are willing to come regularly. If motivation for treatment is unilateral, the marriage is usually doomed. Psychotherapy cannot inspire love afresh. This is a spiritual rather than a psychological problem. Therapy can help, however, in improving communication. This is the crux of both marital and family therapy. Even when love is lost, improved communication between spouses or between them and their children can significantly affect the home for the better. If this can be achieved, love can often be rediscovered.

*Group therapy.* Group therapy is becoming popular and is one of the best answers to the problem of too many patients and too few doctors. It is indicated for those whose psychopathology causes them to fear or distrust individual therapy or in cases of serious antagonism toward parental or authority figures. It is also especially useful for patients with character disorders, general social maladjustment, bad or absent sibling and family relationships, and those having homosexual fears toward the therapist. Children generally do well in group therapy. Patients of low intelligence also do better in peer groups than in individual therapy. Groups consist usually of five to eight members, all of whom have roughly the same socioeconomic backgrounds and have similar problems which they all discuss openly. They are under the leadership of the therapist who intervenes from time to time, for example, to dampen a member who is tending to dominate the group, encourage a more withdrawn member, or protect a vulnerable one in danger of having his defenses exposed by the others. Patients who tend to act out their difficulties do well in groups because they can learn to modify their behavior in the social milieu which the group provides. They soon realize that they are not the only ones with their type of problem, and they begin to verbalize their difficulties to the others as freely as to their therapist when alone. Criticism or advice from peers in the group is often more readily accepted, and therefore acted upon, than when it comes from the therapist. Friendships made in the group can be a significant learning experience for the patient whose problems are in the area of interpersonal relationships. Alcoholics Anonymous, Weight Watchers, and groups established for addicts or homosexuals provide opportunities for sharing and identification with others who have similar problems.

A word of warning about groups convened without professional leadership. Although some encounter groups can be helpful, there is the danger that some inadequately trained group leaders may through inexperience permit destructive interactions to take place which could be harmful to certain members. In particular, sensitivity groups which encourage total exposure of emotional content with no controlling inhibitions allowed can be very damaging to fragile individuals. Nudity groups which encourage bodily contact claim this leads to total honesty, acceptance, and the absence of artificiality and status. In fact, this practice merely destroys the normal personal reserve necessary in the preservation of self-respect and identity.

*Hypnosis.* Hypnosis or hypnotism is a grossly overrated dramatic technique which has some usefulness but is no cure-all. Carefully selected patients, if there is no deep underlying conflict, can be helped to some improvement. Dentists can use it as general anaesthesia for such procedures as fillings and extractions. Habits such as smoking can be broken, a headache can be temporarily cured, mild anxiety calmed, and posthypnotic suggestions can be made to alter certain forms of behavior.

Hypnosis should only be used by physicians or dentists in their fields of professional competence. Medical school is the place to learn it. Hypnotists using the technique for entertainment purposes should be prohibited by law. Do-it-yourself courses by correspondence or on phonograph records should also be outlawed. Improper use by unqualified people can be very dangerous. Even most fully trained psychiatrists do not attempt to use it because of lack of experience. Anyone less qualified who tampers with it is a potential menace.

*Narcotherapy.* Narcotherapy or narcosynthesis is another form of treatment for some special conditions. Amytal or sodium pentothal given in small doses into a vein can act as a sort of "truth drug" and enable the patient to talk about things he might not do when inhibited by full consciousness. This is sometimes helpful in psychotherapy but not necessarily. As every bartender knows you can still lie when you're drunk!

*Aim of psychotherapy.*   Psychotherapy aims at helping the whole man, not just removing his symptoms. Symptoms brought the patient to the psychiatrist, but it is the total personality which needs to be treated. The ultimate aim is to enable the whole man to function successfully and happily in all areas in his job, in his social circle, and in the intimacy of his own home and personal life.

# 14
# CHRISTIAN PSYCHOTHERAPY AND COUNSELING

**How therapist influences treatment.** Some of the principles outlined in chapter 13 can be applied to therapy and counseling within a Biblical framework. Specifically Christian therapy differs from that which has no regard for divine revelation or spiritual power. Unhappily the patient's personal religious or spiritual life is so often overlooked by most psychiatrists. This is not surprising if the psychiatrist himself has no personal faith or belief. Even if he has, the probability is that by training he will keep his religion strictly separate from his therapy or counseling. If he is an unbeliever or an atheist, this is probably just as well, but no therapist is able completely to avoid having his values, ethics, beliefs, and moral standards influence his therapy. He is, after all, being paid to help with problems which involve principles of living which are influenced by both psychological and spiritual factors. His judgments and conclusions about a patient's problems and his opinions and advice to him cannot help but be affected by his own convictions. Although a nonbelieving therapist may claim that he does not bring into his treatment considerations of moral issues of right and wrong, he cannot in fact avoid them. Every day people have to make decisions. They expect their therapist to help with some of them. They usually want to do what is right, not simply that which is temporarily expedient. It does matter, therefore, what the therapist's own views are since he is able to influence decisions which sometimes radically affect people's lives.

*Therapist develops technique best for him.* Until there have been developed empirically validated and generally accepted principles of psychotherapy which can be proven to be more successful than all others in all cases, it is up to the individual therapist to practice in the way he feels is best for his patients. He has to rely on his own conviction that he knows what he is doing and that the technique is best suited to his own personality and talents and therefore will be the most efficient means he can provide to help those who come to see him. As yet there is no one therapeutic technique or theory consistently better than all others. It is therefore my privilege to use in my practice the methods and principles I deem best in my hands for the benefit of my patients. This I have done. My method is a form of Reality Therapy integrated with basic Christian doctrines, and my principles are to be found in the Old and New Testaments which I believe to be inspired by God.

*Reality Therapy* by William Glasser, M.D., a Los Angeles psychiatrist, is published by Harper & Row and is available in any good bookstore. The book came as a breath of fresh air to me after suffering through many months of study of psychoanalytic theory in which I had great difficulty believing. Obviously analytic theory is not all wrong and some psychiatrists use analytic techniques very successfully. To me, however, an ex-math major in high school and trained for five years in surgery, I felt emotionally committed to the belief that two and two make four. In psychoanalysis they often don't. In reality therapy they usually do.

*Glasser's prerequisites to healthy functioning.* Dr. Glasser gives six major principles which radically differ from conventional psychotherapy. To his ideas I have added some of my own which I believe have enabled me to practice a definite "Christian psychotherapy" based on the teachings of the Holy Scriptures. Basic to each of these six principles are the three essential prerequisites to healthy functioning: (a) to be in touch with and respond to reality or the real world around us; (b) to act responsibly in fulfilling our needs without depriving others of the ability to do the same; (c) to know right from wrong and to choose what is right—*reality, responsibility, and righteousness.*

**Major principles of reality therapy.** *1. Mental illness a weakness rather than disease.* Conventional psychiatry sees mental illness as a definite classifiable medical diagnosis to be treated within a set of rules of therapy for each category. Glasser sees it not as illness but a personal weakness manifested by an inability to fulfill one's needs in a responsible way. For a person to believe he is mentally ill may cause him to feel that, therefore, he is not responsible for his actions. This in turn could lead to the patient not becoming sincerely involved with his therapist in the treatment situation.

I partly agree here. I believe that patients are much more to be held responsible for their illnesses than is generally taught in medical school. Even if schizophrenia, mania, depression, and anxiety states are one day shown to be partly of biochemical origin, there still is a certain respect in which the patient has to remain responsible for his handling of the situation. For the same reason, the responsible person is usually better able to deal with his emotional reactions if he is afflicted with some form of mental disturbance than someone who is irresponsible. The Christian has a responsibility to God: "I beseech you therefore, brethren, by the mercies of God, that ye present your bodies [and minds] a living sacrifice, holy, acceptable unto God, which is your reasonable service" (Romans 12:1). In my therapy I strongly emphasize the element of responsibility in daily living and urge the patient if he is a Christian to consider very fully God's claims upon his life. God's will for the Christian is for him to serve God to the utmost of his ability in every facet of life. He can only do this if he is living responsibly.

*2. De-emphasis of searching the past.* Conventional psychiatry teaches that if the patient gains insight and understanding into his past this will lead to change in behavior. As already stated, unhappily, this is just not true, at least not frequently enough to justify the tremendous emphasis in psychoanalytic theory of digging deep into obscure past experiences in the hope that they will explain present feelings or behavior. Glasser further stresses that what is past is past and can never be changed. Past experiences must not be allowed to give patients excuses to avoid present responsibility. In reality therapy present behavior is examined, and needed change is emphasized for the sake of the future. A history is taken by the therapist only to gain the minimal information about the patient's past that he needs to help the patient in the present. The history taking is not for the patient's benefit. He should rather be persuaded to forget the past and should accept it as a historic fact which cannot be changed. For the Christian the past is forgiven and forgotten. It is a sin to dredge up again things that have been once and for all confessed, repented of, and forgiven. ". . . This one thing I do, forgetting those things which are behind, and reaching forth unto those things which are before, I press toward the mark for the prize of the high calling of God in Christ Jesus" (Philippians 3:13, 14).

*3. Involvement better than transference.* One of the cardinal principles of psychoanalysis is that of transference. In this process the patient transfers to the therapist attitudes and feelings he formerly felt toward previous authority figures in his life. Supposedly after the therapist has understood the transference, he explains it to the patient who is then expected to change his attitudes and relate to people in a better way because of the insight he has gained. The transference relationship, however, is a somewhat aloof one, the therapist not giving of himself at all or allowing himself to become deeply involved. I personally went for two years three times each week to an analyst during the period of my psychiatric training. In all that time he never once voluntarily told me anything about himself. Such was his technique. Such was his unwillingness to become involved. He is, however, an excellent therapist and I admit that I derived a lot of help in self-understanding from him. My reaction to him was a curious mixture of hostility and affection. I resented his aloofness but liked him for helping me to straighten out some of the difficulties in my training that I was having at the time.

Reality therapy is very different, however. Dr. Glasser permits himself to discuss very freely a wide variety of subjects with his patients. They are not looking for yet another unsatisfactory relationship, he stresses. They are looking for a warm personal involvement through which they can meet some of their present needs in a satisfying and appropriate manner. I go much further even than Dr. Glasser in this area. I often go for walks with my patients in Central Park; many of them have been out to dinner with me, and many others have visited with me and my wife at home. I have played handball, golf, and squash racquets with one or two and gone to concerts and operas with others. Many of my patients have, of course, had social contact with me at the church where I am a member or at other churches where I have had speaking engagements. In my office I freely talk about myself and my personal life to my patients, in response to their questions, whenever I feel that to share these things will be helpful to them. I believe I am presently living a very full and personally satisfying life professionally, socially, and in my home. Trying to inspire my patients to strive to achieve the same and helping them to do it is in my view good therapy. At no time that I am aware of has mutual respect been damaged because of social contact with my patients. There is no reason why respect should be lost as long as one's behavior is exemplary. In the case of Christian patients, involvement can include reading passages of Scripture and praying out loud together. These I will always do with a patient if he requests it. I have a special relationship with a patient if he is a born-again Christian: "So we, being many, are one body in Christ, and every one members one of another" (Romans 12:5). It is my special privilege as a Christian to help a fellow member in Christ with my God-given training and experience.

**4. *Conscious rather than unconscious probing stressed.*** Analytic theory places much importance on unearthing the unconscious mind through the interpretation of dreams, slips of the tongue, and the products of free association. Unfortunately, as with understanding the past, a knowledge of the unconscious reasons for maladaptive behavior does not necessarily lead to change. As Glasser says: "They still do not change because knowing the reason does not lead to fulfilling needs." He further states that knowledge of the unconscious merely gives the patient more evidence to excuse his inadequate functioning and avoidance of reality. Conscious awareness is necessary to respond to present reality responsibly.

Consider how we sometimes avoid reality: We daydream and fantasize in attempts to forget reality. We project onto others blame we should ourselves acknowledge, and hence we distort reality. The attitude of "sour grapes" is an attempt to distort reality. So also for the Christian is the "sweet lemon" when he distorts it by telling himself that a particular disappointment was only God's will after all. Sometimes we try to compensate for the hard facts of reality. For example, we disparage others so as to appear good ourselves in contrast. We sometimes malinger or regress to a previous area of security to avoid facing a tough reality situation. The sociopath attacks reality by his criminal behavior which he knows full well will get him into trouble. Conversion hysteria or psychosis are retreats from reality. Psychosomatic symptoms often result from not dealing with reality responsibly. Perfectionism and excessive overwork with inadequate rest or vacations are also inappropriate ways of dealing with reality. Understanding the unconscious reasons for all these forms of irresponsible behavior is not going to change the situations but merely provides excuses for them. Conscious involvement with reality has to happen first for any improvement to take place. As Christians we are challenged to renew our minds to bring them into conformity with God's will which is ultimate reality: "And be not conformed to this world: but be ye transformed by the renewing of your mind, that ye may prove what is that good, and acceptable, and perfect, will of God" (Romans 12:2).

**5. *Moral principles stressed.*** As stated previously, moral standards and the issues of right and wrong are not the concerns of conventional psychiatry. Deviant behavior is regarded as the product of mental illness. The criminal is not morally responsible for his crimes. He is a poor, helpless sick person in need of a psychiatrist, not punishment. In fact, the opposite is true. I have frequently asked sociopathic and psychotic patients certain questions to test whether or not their mental condition had adversely affected their knowledge of right and wrong. In every case they answered correctly. Even the seriously mentally ill person still has residual knowledge and the superego or consciously controlled ability to distinguish between morally correct or incorrect courses of action. Where they can fail of course is in the area of emotional control, not in discernment or understanding of the facts at issue. In other words, the criminal may temporarily be emotionally disturbed enough to commit his crime but he *does* know intellectually while he is doing it that it is morally or legally wrong. A rare possible exception may be in the cases of some organic conditions such as epilepsy or brain tumor.

Dr. Glasser makes the point that all society is based on moral and religious principles and that the individual must responsibly judge his own standards of behavior to bring it into conformity with the society in which he lives. As Christians we have absolute standards as our guidelines. The Holy Scriptures are for the Christian a handbook of daily living. They are our guide to what is right and wrong according to God's perfect and holy standard. The Ten Commandments and the Golden Rule are still valid today. So, for the Christian, are several others of the laws of Moses, the Sermon on the Mount, and the admonitions of Paul and the other New Testament writers. "Thy word is a lamp unto my feet, and a light unto my path" (Psalms 119:105). Jesus said: "If ye love me, keep my commandments" (John 14:15).

**6. To teach is better than to be nondirective.** Conventional psychiatry, inasmuch as it is based on psychoanalytic theory, is essentially nondirective. The therapist does not attempt to tell the patient what he should do. His theory is that once the patient understands why things have gone wrong he will change. Insight leads to improved behavior. A nice theory. The only trouble is that it usually does not work. There is a limit to how much I can learn by my mistakes. Yes, sometimes I can learn by them but I will learn very much more quickly and just as thoroughly if I am taught the correct way by someone else who has the right answers. Dr. Glasser makes no apologies for being directive. He admits that he instructs his patients in better ways to fulfill their needs. Reality therapy is unashamedly directive. I wholeheartedly agree. Life is too short to wait for years of probing into all the hundreds of ways I have failed in the past. All I need to do is to humble myself enough to admit that I have made mistakes and failed and then be willing to learn a better way from someone else who can help me to succeed. To be able to help my patients I must first have succeeded myself. Then I can instruct them on how to go and do likewise.

**Christian therapy an opportunity.**    In humility I want to say that I believe that I have succeeded, but not because of some great effort on my part for which I should be congratulated. I have succeeded because of God's gifts to me of my wonderful parents, my home upbringing, my education and training, and my opportunities. God also gave me my personality, my talents, and my ambitions. What is this success anyway? Certainly not my degrees, my standard of living, the esteem of my friends, or even good bodily and mental health, though all of these are also gifts ultimately from God. No, success for the Christian can only be measured in terms of his conformity to the will of God for his life. At the present time I believe before God, with no known barrier between Him and me, that I am where He wants me to be and am doing what He wants me to be doing. This is not sinless perfection, but it *is* an honest attempt, albeit with many failures, to live responsibly and fulfill the purposes for which I was created. If you agree that this is success, then I have the obligation to pass this on to others. As a Christian psychiatrist I have the opportunity to influence men and women for Jesus Christ. Every day I see a dozen troubled souls whom God has brought into my life because He wants me to help them both to get well mentally and also to grow in their relationship to Him. Naturally most of my spiritually oriented dialogue is with patients who already profess to be believing Christians. With them I honestly attempt to integrate sound principles of psychotherapy with the teachings of Scripture. In the case of non-Christian patients, I let them know briefly where I stand but never preach at them. If they show an interest, I do of course then witness freely to them. When I was a zealous new Christian twenty years ago, my present opportunities for Christ would have surpassed my wildest dreams.

*Mediation by the Holy Spirit.*    When I first opened my private office, five minutes before my first patient came, I stood at the door, looking at all my brand new furniture, and thanked God. Then I dedicated myself afresh to Him and committed myself to serving Him faithfully. I prayed for continuing professional competence and asked that my many long years of training would now bring glory to His Son in the changed lives of those He sent me for help. I asked to be kept humble and true to Biblical revelation. I asked to be given the special gift of healing, and I believe that He answered by sending the power of the Holy Spirit into many of my encounters with troubled Christians. Certainly on countless occasions since then I have been conscious of the guidance of the Spirit coming both into my own thoughts and into the thoughts of many patients. The influence of the Spirit in sessions with Christian patients has added a completely new dimension to my therapy which had previously been lacking before that power had been invoked.

I have been used as a confessional by many who needed to unburden their guilt. Sometimes I have functioned as a *pastor pastorum* to some ministers who, wearied by their own efforts in counseling, have come for help themselves. There really *is* something different about Christian psychotherapy if that difference is the additional power and influence of God mediated by the Holy Spirit. As I have increased in confidence and experience I have felt more and more free to integrate Scriptural principles into the strategy and tactics of psychotherapy that I learned while in training. Quoting or reading from the Bible is frequently not only appropriate but often freshly illuminating and helpful to patients. Prayer at the close of a session, spoken by me alone or by both of us, often sends the patient away with a renewed hope for the future and a deep calm and peace within.

Psychiatrists and pastoral counselors have one major thing in common, whatever may be their philosophical or doctrinal differences. They are both concerned with helping people who come to them with problems which are damaging their functioning efficiency or personal happiness. Both have had successes and both have had failures. In attempting myself to combine these approaches, using both the results of good professional training and my personal Christian experience and Scriptural knowledge, I am hoping to deal more fully with the problems in my patients' lives. With God's help I can become a good therapist and a good counselor: a good doctor and a good Christian. I believe this is His will for my life, and my ambition is to achieve it for the benefit of my patients.

# SUGGESTED READING

Adams, Jay E. *Competent to Counsel.* Nutley, N. J.: Presbyterian & Reformed Publishing Co., 1970.

Allen, Charles L. *God's Psychiatry.* Old Tappan, N. J.: Fleming H. Revell Co., 1965.

Cooper, Kenneth H. *The New Aerobics.* New York: Bantam Books, 1970.

Cramer, Raymond L. *The Psychology of Jesus and Mental Health.* Los Angeles: Cowman Publications, Inc., 1959.

Frankl, Viktor E. *Man's Search for Meaning.* New York: Washington Square Press, 1963.

Frazier, S. H., and Carr, Arthur C. *Introduction to Psychopathology.* New York: Macmillan Co., 1964.

Glasser, William. *Reality Therapy.* New York: Harper & Row, 1965.

Green, Hannah. *I Never Promised You a Rose Garden.* New York: Signet Books, 1965.

Kolb, Lawrence C., ed. *Noyes' Modern Clinical Psychiatry.* Philadelphia: W. B. Saunders Co., 1968.

La Haye, Tim. *How to Be Happy Though Married.* Wheaton, Ill.: Tyndale House, 1968.

Lewis, C. S. *The Problem of Pain.* New York: Macmillan Co., 1962.

Little, L. Gilbert. *The Christian and Emotional Problems.* Lincoln, Neb.; Back to the Bible Broadcast, 1970.

McMillen, S. I. *None of These Diseases.* Old Tappan, N. J.: Fleming H. Revell Co., 1963.

Meehl, Paul, et al. *What, Then, Is Man?* St. Louis, Mo.: Concordia Publishing House, 1958.

Menninger, William, and Leaf, Munro. *You and Psychiatry.* New York: Charles Scribner's Sons, 1948.

Narramore, Clyde M. *Encyclopedia of Psychological Problems.* Grand Rapids, Mich.: Zondervan Publishing House, 1966.

Polatin, Philip, and Philtine, Ellen C. *How Psychiatry Helps.* New York: Collier Books, 1965.

Smith, Hannah Whitall. *The Christian's Secret of a Happy Life.* Old Tappan, N. J.: Fleming H. Revell Co., 1952.

Tournier, Paul. *Guilt and Grace.* New York: Harper & Row, 1962.

Tweedie, Jr., Donald F. *The Christian and the Couch.* Grand Rapids, Mich.: Baker Book House, 1963.

White, Ernest. *Christian Life and the Unconscious.* New York: Harper & Row, 1955.

# INDEX OF SCRIPTURE REFERENCES

# INDEX